The UX Five-Second Rules

The UX Five-Second Rules

Guidelines for User Experience Design's Simplest Testing Technique

Paul Doncaster

AMSTERDAM • BOSTON • HEIDELBERG • LONDON
NEW YORK • OXFORD • PARIS • SAN DIEGO
SAN FRANCISCO • SINGAPORE • SYDNEY • TOKYO

Morgan Kaufmann is an imprint of Elsevier

Morgan Kaufmann is an imprint of Elsevier
225 Wyman Street, Waltham, MA, 02451, USA

First published 2014

British Library Cataloguing-in-Publication Data
A catalogue record for this book is available from the British Library

Library of Congress Cataloging-in-Publication Data
A catalog record for this book is available from the Library of Congress

ISBN: 978-0-12-800534-7

For information on all MK publications
visit our website at www.mkp.com

This book has been manufactured using Print On Demand technology. Each copy is produced to order and is limited to black ink. The online version of this book will show color figures where appropriate.

ELSEVIER **Book Aid** International

Working together
to grow libraries in
developing countries

www.elsevier.com • www.bookaid.org

CONTENTS

At a time when business stakeholders are buying in to the idea of leveraging user involvement to create, iterate, validate, and optimize user interface designs, the online five-second test offers an almost-too-good-to-be-true proposition for designers and researchers. By making tests public and leveraging social media, large samples of data can be collected from actual or prospective users, often for little or no monetary investment, in a relatively short amount of time. The tool available at UsabilityHub.com, with its innovative "karma points" model, ups the ante by allowing account holders to earn credits for their own tests by taking part in the tests of others—a virtual "win-win" situation for everybody.

The impetus for this book was the author's participation in dozens of such tests, grounded in a sincere effort to assist fellow designers and user experience professionals. With each test taken, it became increasingly clear that many researchers were likely not getting the information they were hoping for due to a fundamental misunderstanding of the method and what it can and cannot do well. Further, there appeared to be precious little information available about how to get the most out of the method using these online, unmoderated tools, nor were there any established guidelines or principles for structuring tests to get the best possible data.

This books aims to fill that knowledge gap by taking a holistic view of the method as it currently exists and with consideration to the impact that online, unmoderated tools now have on it. It will also challenge some of the restrictions and limitations of the method originators and, hopefully, spark a reconsideration of what the method can accomplish:

- Chapter 1 will introduce and define the method, describe its origins in the lab setting, and examine how it is being used currently based on a sample of more than 300 online tests that were collected between April and September of 2012.

- Chapter 2 will present a set of guiding principles, or "rules," for constructing effective five-second tests, from distinguishing proper and improper uses of the method to approaches for maximizing each specific element of a test.
- Chapters 3 and 4 will discuss specialized attitudinal topics that are prevalent in five-second testing and will provide templates for testing these aspects.
- Chapter 5 will offer examples of how to stretch the method to test designs beyond those of web pages and individual design elements intended for web pages (which make up the vast majority of current tests).

The author wishes to acknowledge and thank Jen McGinn and Dr. Deborah J. Mayhew for their invaluable (and much appreciated) insights and guidance toward the completion of this book, and to the following for their contributions to its inspiration and development: Michael Hawley, Whitney Quesenbery, Christine Perfetti, Tom Tullis, Jared Spool, the entire UXPA community, Tristan Gamilis, Matt Milosavljevic and Alan Downie of UsabilityHub.com, Meg Dunkerly and Heather Scherer of Morgan Kaufman Publishing. Special heartfelt thanks to Kim Doncaster for her sustaining love and support.

CHAPTER *1*

The Method

Over time—and with the emergence of technology providers who wish to capitalize on its potential value as a research tool—the method being examined in this book has come to be known by more than one name. For example, the Verify suite of design apps developed by ZURB refers to it as a "memory test," while UserZoom's testing software calls it a "screenshot timeout test." In deference to those who created and first implemented it (Perfetti, 2005), this book will refer to it by its original name: the "five-second test." Before delving into the actual guidelines for constructing successful tests, it is important to understand the characteristics of the method, how it has evolved since its initial implementation as a lab-based exercise, and how current trends in its usage point to the need for test design guidelines.

1.1 WHAT IS A FIVE-SECOND TEST?

The five-second test is actually a type of survey methodology—a variation on the simple act of asking questions and getting responses in return. In the business world, surveys are most frequently used by marketers, product managers, and corporate strategists to gauge current attitudes and opinions about a product or service, then use that data to both uncover current trends and project future trends. In the world of user experience (UX) and design research, in which there is so much focus on behavioral activity, surveys are commonly used both in the early stages of a project, before pen is ever taken to paper (to create user profiles, uncover preferences, etc.), and postlaunch, to measure reactions to a product and gather relevant demographics on who's using it and how.

The five-second test, on the other hand, is a type of survey used to help develop a design while in its formative stages. The critical difference in terms of both approach and structure is that marketing or political surveys typically involve giving answers about a topic or issue about which participants have prior knowledge or about a previous experience having taken place more than a few minutes prior to the survey—in other words, experiences that leverage long-term memory in order to recall and respond. Conversely, five-second tests require little reliance on prior knowledge: pretty much everything is "in the moment," confined largely to the processes of visual perception and short-term memory. Despite the noted differences, five-second tests share a key similarity with traditional surveys: if not designed carefully, each is fully capable of producing results that are inaccurate, inconclusive, and/or deceptive.

Compared to other UX and design research methods, conducting a five-second test is about as simple as it gets: A test participant is given a set of instructions, views an image of a design for a few seconds, and answers questions about it. That's it. This simplicity in execution means that the five-second test has a number of advantages in its favor:

- **Speed:** A test conducted "in-person" can be administered to a participant in as little as 5 min. Online tests can take less than that.
- **Efficiency:** Because they are quick to administer, five-second tests can produce comparatively large result sets in a short amount of time. Even when administered one-on-one in a lab setting (assuming no other types of research are included), a researcher could reasonably accommodate up to 30–40 participants or more in an 8-h day. Using tools that leverage crowdsourcing (as noted in the Preface) or allow for the distribution of participation links via social media can extend that capability much further.
- **Portability:** Five-second tests can be run in virtually any environment that contains willing participants. In-person moderated tests can be performed using printouts of a design and pen-and-paper, or on any portable computer device that can display an image. Online tests require only access to the online tool and a valid test URL.
- **Flexibility:** Five-second tests can be unique and distinct research exercises focused on a single design question, or they can be (and are most often are) included as components of a larger design or UX study.

Much of this book will describe the specific limitations of the method, but its biggest limitation is one that is shared by all UX and design research methods: *It can't tell you everything.* Using the method effectively requires the acceptance that it is good for only certain types of research questions, and at best supplies only one piece of a potentially large puzzle. With that understood, the five-second test can be counted on to be a useful addition to any researcher's toolkit.

The nature of the method, as well as its name, begs the question: Why 5 s? Is there some definable advantage to that amount of time which makes it ideal for this type of research? There doesn't seem to be a clear-cut answer to that question, as attempts to find origins in the psychological and physiological literature have not provided a verifiable link to the method as we know it. However, calculated cycle times within the Model Human Processor (Card et al., 1983) indicate that the rates at which items—colors, words, shapes, etc.—can be matched against working memory range anywhere from 27 to 93 s per item, depending on the type. It would therefore follow that 5 s (5000 ms) would allow the viewer enough time to commit a good number of elements to working memory and accommodate the method's goals of reporting both visual prominence and memorability. If a design is shown for less than 5 s, a participant may take in a lot of information perceptually, but likely does not have time to make much sense of it as a whole entity, resulting in feedback that is limited in scope. If a design is shown for more than 5 s, a participant may move beyond the perceptual and view a page more critically, giving longer consideration times to other aspects of the design and moving away from the original areas of focus.

1.2 THE PROCESSES IN PLAY

As noted earlier, five-second tests are different than traditional surveys in that they gauge responses to a direct visual stimulus. This difference means that there are a number of cognitive processes in play during each phase of a test which are not in play during traditional surveys. These processes impact each other and make it critical that cognitive resources are maximized in ways that traditional surveys do not require. It is certainly beyond the scope of this book to provide a full accounting of the psychological processes in play; however, a very quick review of the relevant high-level concepts would be helpful in providing background information for the types of issues that the five-second rules seek to address:

- Viewing the test image within the 5 s limit represents a large emphasis on **perception**, or the organization, identification, and interpretation of sensory information—in this case, visual information—in order to understand and make sense of the environment. This process seems mostly effortless, because it occurs outside of conscious awareness; however, it involves complex functions of the nervous system which handle the information about what we see and manages the relations between objects and images.

- The testing of finished web page designs means that multiple elements visible at the same time in a single eye scan will compete for the viewer's attention. Two processes work together to process and make sense of these sets of visual stimuli: **bottom-up (stimulus-driven) mechanisms** deal with perception, while **top-down (knowledge-driven)** processes deal with prior knowledge and memory (Albers, 2012). Both play a role in how the mind attends to items present in the environment.

- During the 5 s that the image is displayed, information is being built up in the viewer's **short-term memory** store, which holds everything a person is capable of thinking of at any particular moment. How many things a human can commit to memory and recall at any given time is a subject of ongoing debate, but it's typically regarded as seven, plus or minus two (Miller, 1956), and the cognitive tasks involved in completing a five-second test can erode that number even further. By its very nature, short-term memory—sometimes referred to as **working memory**—is temporary and transitory: as new stimuli are received and reactions are initiated, working memory is "reset" to make room for the next set of information (Baddeley and Hitch, 1974).

- The introduction of other cognitive tasks (reading a question, formulating an answer, entering the answer, moving on to the next) after the test image is removed requires a shift to **explicit memory**, or the conscious memory of previous actions and information which people can recall as needed (Albers, 2012). Recall and recognition require the participant to think back to whatever information about the image has been stored in memory.

- Throughout the latter phases of the test, working memory is constantly shifting between the recall of the design and attending to answering the test questions, causing interference and decay of the working memory (Card et al., 1983). What we will hereafter refer to as **memory fade**, relative to the original image, can increase frustration and/or impact how test questions are handled, such that some will become difficult to answer.

The "Reverse Polaroid" Effect

To consider how this all comes together for participants in a five-second test, let's reference a technology which at one time was futuristic but is now a historic cultural curiosity: the Polaroid instant picture. First introduced in 1972, the concept was revolutionary: instead of shipping photographs to a lab for processing or each individual film envelope contained all the chemical layers to expose, develop, and fix the photo. After snapping the shot, the photo would eject from the camera, and the image would slowly reveal itself over a span of 60 or so seconds. Within this context, consider the case of a person being asked to describe specifics about the image as it developed. (S)he would be able to provide very few details about it within the first 15–30 s, then gradually have the ability to report the appearance of form outlines and the relative locations of elements within the scene, followed soon thereafter by definable object details and colors, and so on. Upon full completion of the process, the person would be able to describe the image contents with great precision.

What happens in a five-second test is akin to the Polaroid development process taking place in reverse (Figure 1.1), not within the realm of visual perception, but within the different human memory systems. Under this scenario, a fully "developed" image is presented and committed to whatever can be retained in short-term memory. Thereafter, with the introduction of new information entering short-term memory (e.g., reading a test question, considering the response, providing feedback, moving on to the next question), the distinctness of detail slowly is gradually eroded, until a point is reached in which little detail can be recalled. Five-second tests can be effective despite this effect, but their ability to deliver good results requires that test planners take this effect into account, understand the potential impacts, and structure their tests such that the negative impacts on data can be minimized.

0 s   60 s

Figure 1.1 The "reverse Polaroid" effect.

1.3 EVOLUTION: FROM THE LAB TO ONLINE

The earliest instances of the test as a UX method can be traced back to the collaborative efforts of Perfetti et al. (2013). The method was bourne out of necessity, when it became apparent that there were some notable problems with some of the site's **content pages**—pages which typically serve a single purpose and feature a specific type of high-value information. (A common and familiar example of a content page is the "Contact Us" page, which exists solely to provide all of the communications channels—mailing addresses, e-mail addresses, phone numbers, chat links, etc.—needed to contact a business.) Content pages represent the "end of the road" in the search for information and will usually contain the information a user has set out to find. Ultimately, content pages provide the most value to the user, so it is critical that their purpose is understood immediately and that the most important information is communicated optimally. Depending on the nature of the information, the consequences of poorly designed content pages can range from minor user confusion and irritation to reduced conversion rates and lost revenue.

Perfetti et al. set out to see whether the quality of their content pages could be measured with some degree of reliability. Using a modification to the traditional task-based usability test, they devised a very simple set of steps to determine whether the purpose of a content page was obvious or not (Perfetti, 2013):

1. **Establish the test context:** After setting the test participants at ease and communicating the reasons why the research is being conducted, give them a focused task representative of something they would actually do on the page (e.g., look for a specific type of information with the intent of taking an action).
2. **Present the instructions:** Inform the participants that a page will be displayed for 5 s, after which it will be taken away. Ask them to remember as much as possible of what they see, within the context of the focused task.
3. **Display the entire page for 5 s**, then remove it.
4. **Document the recollections:** When prompted, have the participants either write down or verbalize everything they remember about the page. (Having them write the items may assist in thought-collection and initiate additional recollections.)

5. **Get success verification:** Ask the participants one or two specific questions, designed to assess whether (a) the task was accomplished and (b) the page's purpose was apparent.

Once a sample of responses is collected, the page is deemed to be validated if participants can both identify the critical information points and accurately state the page's purpose. If the results show a failure on either count, design teams can use the data to reconsider the page and make changes to ensure that the critical information is more apparent and understandable.

Under these original guidelines, use of the method was limited in the following ways:

- **Focus:** The originators never strayed from focusing on content pages and the obviousness of their purpose. Home pages, for example, were deemed off-limits for this method because of the varied purposes a home page can have, depending on the motivations and information needs of the person visiting it. More specific design aspects (visual appeal, perceived usability, etc.) were likewise considered to be ill-suited for the method's protocols because they strayed from the focus on content (Perfetti, 2013).
- **Applicability of results:** Five-second tests were never regarded as stand-alone means for making design decisions, because they can tell only a small portion of a much larger story. While results can indicate whether or not a page's purpose is understood, it cannot indicate whether a task can be successfully completed on that page once undertaken by the user—that obviously requires interaction with the page. Five-second tests were always used as part of a larger usability study, rather than having the study consist solely of five-second tests. In fact, they were frequently included between tasks while performing a formal usability test, primarily to address a specific research question, but also break up the monotony that can be inherent in traditional usability lab tests.
- **Execution:** Because they were usually included in larger lab-based studies, the early five-second tests were always administered in a controlled environment, with a moderator present—never in an unmoderated/uncontrolled environment or by using remote testing tools. This was done to better manage the participants themselves and the testing variables, which in turn would better ensure the reliability of the data.

Of course, at the time of the method's creation, remote and unmoderated testing options were not nearly as advanced and varied as they are today. Fast-forward 10 or so years, and suddenly a number of companies are offering free or fee-based online tools for designing and executing some variation on the original five-second test. The availability and proliferation of these tools have contributed to increases in the method's usage: UsabilityHub alone reports that more than 100,000 unique five-second tests are completed on its site in a calendar year.

However, a closer look at how these tools are promoted indicates a distinct movement away from some of Perfetti et al.'s original guidelines specific to focusing on content pages. UsabilityHub, for example, promotes its tool as ideal for testing the understandability of *landing pages.* (Definitions can vary, but a landing page is typically defined as any page which exists to facilitate an important conversion action within a web site (Ash et al., 2012).) Likewise, UserZoom notes the method as useful for optimizing *landing page* conversion. Neither site makes any reference to limiting use of the method to content pages, nor do they recommend its use as being especially effective for content pages. There is also a notable exclusion of the method as a means of validating the clarity of a page's purpose. In light of the emphasis on landing pages, this omission makes sense, as the purpose of any page with an information entry form on it is bound to be self-evident. Instead, the promotional text for these tools is heavy with references to measuring the memorability of elemental specifics (marketing messages, calls to action, and the like), visual prominence, perceptual likes and dislikes, and aesthetic appeal.

The sample of tests analyzed for this book indicates that users of the tools are using them in line with the marketing efforts of the providers. It shows that the method is being used to test a wide variety of page types, as well as individual logos and icons, comparison of design elements, and for other "nonstandard" uses. This may be due, at least in part, to a fundamental misunderstanding of (or disregard for) the original intent and structure of the method. More likely, it is a reflection of the method's perceived strengths—by limiting the amount of exposure to a design and eliciting gut-level reactions to them, the method's usefulness seems ideally suited for going beyond the original scope of content page and clearness of page purpose, and moving into measuring emotional response, identification of specific visual elements, etc. on all types of pages and designs. Whatever the explanation may be, it is a fact that UX and design professionals are using these tools to employ the method in new and varied ways—*the issue is whether or not users understand how to use the tools optimally to get the data they need.*

1.4 WHAT'S GOING WRONG?

To some ways, the online unmoderated five-second test may be a victim of its own perceived simplicity and relative cost-effectiveness. A perhaps inevitable outcome of the promise of design feedback delivered quickly and cheaply is that tools are made available to inexperienced researchers who have little or no knowledge of good research design and technique. It also could be that more experienced researchers are being lulled into a sense of laziness when it comes to test construction. One need only to participate in a few public tests (you can do so at www.fivesecondtest.com) to see that the opportunity for improvement is large indeed. The following are admittedly egregious examples of what one can expect to see.

Example 1: Promotional Products
Instructions: "Imagine that you are looking for promotional products" (Figure 1.2)

Q1. "What does the company do?"
Q2. "What do you think the purpose of this web site is?"
Q3. "Does this web site grab your attention?"
Q4. "How would you improve this site?"
Q5. "Does this design compel you to call [the company]?"

Why it's a Bad Test
- The instructions ask the participant to put him or herself in a context that most likely is unfamiliar or unreasonable. In a perfect world, participants would be limited to people who do indeed research and procure promotional products, but as this is a crowdsourced test, the likelihood of a respondent fitting that profile is remote, so the context statement adds little practical value. More importantly, in a test that focuses largely on interpretation of and reaction to the page's visual design, the context statement adds little value toward setting the proper expectation for answering the questions that will follow.

Figure 1.2 Promotional products web site home page.

- The image requires the participant to scroll, both horizontally and vertically, in order to see anything other than the company name, some of the navigation, and a portion of a very large photo. Presenting the page in this way reduces the amount of time participants can focus their attention to the image as a whole in order to provide meaningful and useful answers. When that amount of time is limited to 5 s, maximizing every microsecond of attention is critical.
- Q1 and Q2 both represent wasted opportunities to get useful data. Because the intructions explicitly state that the product or service of the web site is the sale and distrubution of promotional products, the vast majority of answers to these first two questions are almost guaranteed to be "the company sells promotional products" and "the purpose is to sell promotional products."
- Q3 is, in most cases, a weak question. For one thing, from the standpoint of the participant taking the test, there is little choice but to have his/her attention grabbed, because it's the only design presented. If, as would appear to be the case here, the purpose for its inclusion is to determine whether or not the page's *design* is engaging and appealing, the question can be worded to better facilitate the desired type of feedback. (On the other hand, if the intent of the test is to measure the positive or negative effect of one visual design

choice—color scheme, layout, etc.—versus one tested in a separate research exercise, it could be viable to include.) Finally, the question is phrased to elicit a "yes" or "no" answer, the truthfulness of which cannot be verified—just because somebody indicates that something is so, doesn't mean it is. A different wording strategy can give more precise meaning to this type of question.

- Q4 represents an unreasonable request on the part of the researcher. Given the limited amount of time the image is in view, and especially given that the test image presents only a portion of the entire page, the ability of a participant to identify problem areas and offer alterntive solutions is very limited. In the best-case scenario, this question could elicit negative qualitative data (e.g., "the stripey thing in the photo is really freaky") that might prove useful; but only if enough responses reference the same element.
- Like the instructions, Q5 assumes that participants can place them-selves in a context that is somewhat familiar—again, this is fine if they have been recruited against a specific persona, but in crowd-sourced testing, the likelihood is remote. Combine that factor with the "yes/no" question issue seen in Q3, and you have a recipe for highly unreliable data.

Example 2: Internships
Instructions: "This is our home page. The most important things I will ask you to keep in mind are the 'professionalism' of the page and its clarity. Thank you very much!" (Refer to Figure 1.3.)

Q1. "Is the page clear? (not overloaded with unnecessary information or pictures, etc?)"

Q2. "Can you tell what is our activity just having looked at this page for 5 s?"

Q3. "Is the page nice looking to you as an Internet user? Does it look attractive and make you want to continue navigate on our web site?"

Q4. "There is a banner with pictures at the top of the page. Since we are a company that provides internships, cultural stays, languages courses in Prague, should the pictures be about people who were our customers or pictures of Prague instead?"

Q5. "What did you like? What changes would you make?"

Figure 1.3 International internship website home page.

Why it's a Bad Test

- As in Example 1, the image requires vertical scrolling to see the entire picture. While scrolling may not be necessary to answer the upcoming questions, the participant cannot assume or predict that. The mere presence of a scrollable bar can tempt participants to explore other parts of the page, which can interfere with retention of details needed to render opinions about professionalism and page clarity.

- Q1 correctly references back to the "clarity" expectation set in the instructions and is specific to the page's *design* clarity (i.e., free of clutter), as opposed to whether the page's *purpose* is clearly understood. So far, so good.

- Q2 is related to clarity but suffers from the same "yes/no" question deficiency we've seen elsewhere. Changing the question to "What does this organization do?" or "What activity are we involved in?" will guide the participant toward giving a more precise answer, which will provide a much more meaningful data set and, if there are misconceptions, point to possible solutions for rectifying them.

- Q3 represents a common violation of survey design. It appears to contain two questions (usually a no-no in any type of survey research), but in fact there are three. The second half is actually a **double-barrel question**, one that touches upon more than one issue, yet allows only for one answer. Just because a participant may think the page is attractive does not necessarily mean that (s)he would want to continue navigating through the site. As in the previous example, this question aims to gauge the page design's aesthetic appeal; there are more effective means of getting this type of data.

- Q4 asks the user to recall a specific element on the page, which is challenging after having processed and answered the previous questions. It's very likely that the participant has forgotten what existed there, which makes it that much more difficult to render an opinion. Also, it's a very long question to read, which acts to further deplete the memory of the image shown.
- Aside from being another example of two questions in a single instance, Q5 is a variation on the "how would you improve" question in Example 1. Here again, given the limited amount of time the participant has to consider the design, it is not an optimal scenario for soliciting specific recommendations. Thoughtful consideration of design and verbalizing recommendations requires time, as well as an appropriate mechanism for detailed feedback, neither of which are afforded in a web-based five-second test.

Example 3: The Donate Button
Instructions: "Find the donate button!" (Figure 1.4).

Q1. "What is the purpose of this page?"
Q2. "Use one word to describe the design of the page."
Q3. "Were you able to find the donate button?"
Q4. "Would you be interested in joining IAVA?"
Q5. "What benefits does the IAVA offer?"

Why it's a Bad Test
- Five-second testing is not optimal for this type of research. Other methods, such as formal usability testing or eye tracking, would be more appropriate. If resources are limited and/or a "quick check" of the UI is needed to settle an internal dispute, a web-based click test—which indicates where users click on an interface and, in some cases, will indicate how long it took for them to find the target and perform the click—would provide a much more meaningful answer to the research question. But let's proceed with the test analysis anyway.

Figure 1.4 Veterans' organization website home page.

- The instructions call for the participant to do one thing and one thing only—find the donate button. The participant has implicitly been given permission to ignore everything else in the quest to find it.
- Once again, we have a large image that will require scrolling, but in this case it may not pose a problem, as questioning is limited to finding the donate button.
- Given the nature of the instructions and the focus on finding a single visual, the answer to Q1 is pretty much predetermined: "the purpose is to donate money." The participant may well not even be aware that the organization is a charity for American veterans and their families.
- Q2 likewise deviates from the expectation set by the instructions. Having spent the entire 5 s looking for the donate button (and scrolling the page to do it), it is very likely that the participant has paid little attention to visual design.
- Q3 is the only question that relates to the expectation set in the instructions, so within the test context, it should be asked first. Even so, as worded in this test, it will beg the "yes" or "no" answer which, as we've seen in each of the examples thus far, results in data that cannot be verified.

- Q4 is not related to the page or its design. More importantly, it works only in a test comprised of participants who fit a specific profile.
- Q5 asks for the recall of specifics and details about the page's content. We've already established that the quest for the donate button would likely preclude any retention of other page elements. However, this question stretches credulity even further because answering it requires the reading of copy, which cannot be accomplished in most five-second tests. Finally, factual questions about site specifics should be placed earlier in the test, when memory of the test image is sharpest; by placing this question at the end of the test, memory of specifics will have faded to the point where a nonresponse is extremely likely.

Sample Analysis

The corpus analyzed for this book consisted of 319 public online tests, collected over a period of 5 months using the UsabilityHub tool (www.fivesecondtest.com). As noted in the Preface, the site's "karma points" model allows account holders to participate in the tests of others while building up credits to use in their own tests. For each test in which the author participated during this period, the tested image was "grabbed" during its exposure time on-screen using a screen capture program. Likewise, the test instructions and questions were copied and pasted into a spreadsheet. After capturing and recording all elements as described, each test was analyzed individually, with each detected problem designated as a "violation" and placed into a descriptive category. The violation categories included (but were not limited to) the following:

- Inappropriateness of the method, based on types of questions asked
- Test instructions that confuse, misguide, or do not set the proper expectation(s)
- Very large test images that force the user to scroll vertically and/or horizontally to see the entire image
- Content-dense images or pages that place cognitive burden on the viewer
- Inefficient ordering of response questions
- Questions that encourage the "I don't know" or "I can't remember" nonresponse

- Questions that are too lengthy or that encourage overly lengthy responses
- Questions that attempt to cover too many different design aspects within a single test.

When all was said and done, more than 75% of the tests were determined to have at least two violations. A simple severity scale was devised to categorize each of the tests into an "offender" status. The resulting breakdown is as follows:

- 18% of the tests had four or more violations (extreme offender)
- 30% had three violations (moderate offender)
- 28% had two violations (minor offender)
- Only 24% of the tests contained only one violation, or none at all, thus escaping "offender" status. The tests with no violations—only 6% of the overall total—typically consisted of a single question.

A notable finding in this analysis is the fact that 25% of the tests were clearly using the wrong method to get the answers the researchers were looking for, based on the questions they were asking. However, even when those tests were removed from the sample, the violation percentages were roughly the same (Figure 1.5).

It was against this backdrop—an apparent misunderstanding of the method and/or the unique considerations of utilizing it with online,

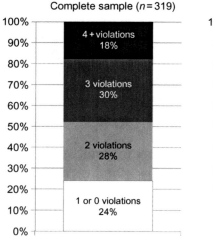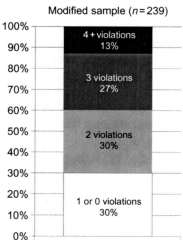

Figure 1.5 Violation analysis of the tests in the corpus.

unmoderated tools—that the "five-second rules" were developed. The intent from this point forward is to focus on maximizing the employment of the five-second test using these unmoderated tools. The rules are based on analysis of the corpus and, in some cases, the results of low-sample tests designed solely to illustrate concepts or test premises laid out in the rules. All research and analysis for the rules was conducted independently for the purposes of this book.

REFERENCES

Albers, M.J., 2012. Human–Information Interaction and Technical Communication. Information Science Reference, Hershey, PA.

Ash, T., Page, R., Ginty, M., 2012. Landing Page Optimization. John Wiley & Sons, Indianapolis, IN.

Baddeley, A.D., Hitch, G., 1974. Working memory. Psychol. Learn. Motiv. 8, 47–89.

Card, S.K., Moran, T.P., Newell, A., 1983. The Psychology of Human–Computer Interaction. L. Erlbaum Associates, Hillsdale, NJ.

Miller, G.A., 1956. The magical number seven, plus or minus two: some limits on our capacity for processing information. Psychol. Rev. 63 (2), 81.

Perfetti, C., 2005. 5-Second Tests: Measuring Your Site's Content Pages Uie.com [online]. Available from: <http://www.uie.com/articles/five_second_test/> (accessed 31.01.13.).

Perfetti, C., 2013. Interview on Five-Second Testing. Interviewed by Paul Doncaster [by phone]. 1 February 2013.

RECOMMENDED READING

Nielsen, J., 2009. "Short-Term Memory and Web Usability" Useit.com [online]. Available from: <http://www.useit.com/alertbox/short-term-memory.html> (accessed 31.01.13.).

Preuss, S., 2011. Five Second Tests: Measure Content Usability and Get a First Impression in Five Seconds. Seibert Media Weblog [blog]. 1 June 2011. Available from: <http://blog.seibert-media.net/2011/06/01/five-second-tests-measure-content-usability-and-first-impression/> (accessed 01.05.13.).

Sauro, J., 2010. 5 Second Usability Tests. Measuring Usability Blog [blog]. 9 November 2010. Available from: <http://www.measuringusability.com/five-second-tests.php> (accessed 19.07.13.).

Spool, J., 2007. Usability Tools Podcast: 5-Second Usability Tests [podcast]. 10 September 2007. Available from: <http://media.rawvoice.com/uie_podcasts/p/www.uie.com/BSAL/UIEUsabilityTools4-5SecTests.mp3> (accessed 20.01.13.).

CHAPTER 2

The UX Five-Second Rules

This set of guidelines offers recommendations on how to effectively construct and conduct online five-second tests, using the tools currently available. They are intended to help the researcher:

- Determine when it is the correct method to use
- Design a test according to the type of data that needs to be collected
- Increase the likelihood of getting useful data sets

While all of the tools reviewed for this book accommodate the basic characteristics and components of the original method (see Chapter 1), each has its own unique set of features, technical capabilities, and limitations. The goal of these guidelines is to provide design research strategies that the researcher can implement regardless of which specific tool is chosen.

The Five-Second Rules

1. Don't use a five-second test when a different research method will produce better results for you (Section 2.1).
2. Focus on the specific design aspect(s) you want to test and employ the appropriate test format (Section 2.2).
3. Don't give participants any excuse to say "I don't know" or "I don't remember" (Section 2.3).
4. Devote time to crafting proper instructions (Section 2.4).
5. Optimize the test image so that scrolling is eliminated (Section 2.5).
6. There is no "magic number" for how many questions to ask, but fewer is usually better (Section 2.6).
7. Order the questions optimally (Section 2.7).
8. Pay careful attention to how the questions are worded (Section 2.8).
9. Ask the "most prominent element" question with discretion (Section 2.9).
10. Open-ended feedback requests carry a high risk of nonresponses and low-information answers (Section 2.10).

2.1 PROPER USE OF THE METHOD

A classic advertising slogan stressed the importance of always having "the right tool for the right job." UX and design researchers inherently understand the importance of this concept; while budget and resources will always loom large in decisions on research, generally speaking the method employed will depend on the goals of the researcher. Unfortunately, another old saying goes: "If all you have is a hammer, everything looks like a nail." As noted in Chapter 1, in many cases, the five-second test has become a victim of its own perceived simplicity and relative cost-effectiveness. Whether it's due to a lack of resources, laziness, or a misunderstanding of what the method is good for, many researchers are opting to use the five-second test as a quick-and-dirty substitute for other types of research that require either longer exposure times or formal interaction with an actual working system or prototype.

Chapter 1 also discussed the emphasis on the perceptual cues and the human capacities in short-term memory that are inherent in five-second tests. These limitations immediately disqualify the method as a means of testing many aspects of UX and visual design. In perhaps the most obvious example, positioning a five-second test around the usability of a page or web site is doomed from the start. Usability speaks to the ability to successfully complete tasks within the context of realistic scenarios; by definition, this requires some degree of meaningful interaction with a working site or a prototype. In a five-second test, a question such as "How would you get information about the highlighted product?" limits the user's options to only what's perceptible in a screenshot, when the task may in fact be easily completed after hovering over the highlighted product and initiating a contextual help box.

In short, five-second testing can test many things, but not everything. As a planning strategy, the rule of thumb should be obvious: *The five-second test is the wrong choice for anything requiring more than five seconds' worth of exposure in order to provide a meaningful answer.* While application of this rule should be fairly straightforward, there are a number of instances in which appropriateness of the method should be called into question, and alternative approaches should be considered.

Reading Text

Always remember that five-second testing is designed to gauge what the viewer can perceive and recall within a very short amount of time.

With a time restriction understood at the outset, the participant's cognitive systems will instinctively race to take in as much of the overall design as possible—perceiving colors and sizes of elements, establishing visual patterns, filling the short-term memory with whatever small amounts of information can be retained—before the visual is taken away. When text is included within the context of an entire web page design, only the text which receives special formatting (extra large fonts, bold or italicized styling, complimentary use of white space, etc.) has a chance of being noticed in a span of 5 s. All other text will undoubtedly be ignored.

Consider the example of a test for the landing page for a skill-sharing service (Figure 2.1). The test instructions noted only that "This is a sign-up page for a new web application." After posing three questions related to the service offered and the background image, the test asked: "Do you have any suggestions on the copy?" The "copy" in this case refers to 46 words in the middle of the page, promoting the service and explaining its general benefit. With all of the other elements competing for attention within the limited amount of exposure time, it is extremely unlikely that any respondent will have enough time to even notice this text, much less internalize, comprehend, and consider it fully enough to render a meaningful opinion (especially when memory capacity has been already been spent answering other questions).

Figure 2.1 Skill-sharing web site landing page.

Reading involves additional, higher level cognitive processes that are better tested by other methods that are not subject to a time limit. However, it could be argued that there are ways to ask about "copy" or "content" without requiring actual reading. Some tests have taken the approach of asking "Does this web site make you want to read on?" or "Would you like to read it further if you had the chance?" However, these questions imply a greater interest in the overall design of the site or page (i.e., "Is the design appealing enough to make you want to explore it further?"). Focusing on whether the "copy" is interesting or engaging would require some level of meaningful attention, which cannot be accomplished within a five-second test.

There is one viable use of the method in cases involving reading: the testing of slogans or taglines for marketing or public relations purposes. Short sentences or phrases of no more than 10–12 words can be read and internalized adequately within a five-second time frame, giving respondents ample opportunity to provide their interpretation of, opinion about, and/or reaction to them. This approach requires that the test be fairly precise in approach and execution. To illustrate, consider the case of a business wanting to test a slogan for a new product:

- The test instructions should specify that the participant will be required to read as part of the test: "You are about to view a slogan proposed for a specific business. Read it carefully in the time provided." This sets the proper expectation and helps ensure that the participant is focused on the task.
- The test image containing the slogan should be removed entirely from the design context. Simple black text on a white background, in large letters and using a common font style like Helvetica or Times New Roman, will help ensure that the slogan is as easy to read as possible, and that the participant isn't biased by a like or dislike of the font style or color.
- Questions should be limited to those measuring interpretation of, opinion about, or reaction to the slogan; for example: "What type of product or service comes to mind when you see this slogan?," "How catchy would you say the slogan is?," or "What does the slogan mean to you?" To test whether the slogan is memorable, you could also ask respondents to recreate the slogan as best they can. (This approach is most effective when the question is asked last in a sequence—it would prove how memorable the slogan really is.)

Design Comparisons

A test focusing on a web site for a provider of elderly care services (Figure 2.2) asked participants the following questions:

Q1. "What services does the company on the right provide?"
Q2. "What services does the company on the left provide?"
Q3. "Which one is more professional? Why?"
Q4. "Which one would you feel more comfortable contacting? Why?"
Q5. "What would be your preferred method of contact for either company?"

Based on these questions, the goals of the researcher appear to be determining (a) which design option more effectively emphasizes the services offered by the company, (b) which design is more professional-looking and visually pleasing, and (c) which design more effectively positions the company as a trusted services provider. It is possible for these three goals to be achieved by running individual tests for each option, then analyzing and comparing the results. They are next to impossible to achieve when two options are presented side-by-side in a single test.

As already noted, the five-second test leverages the primary perceptual cues given by a visual stimulus. The demand on short-term memory is high enough when considering a single design. When attention is

Figure 2.2 Test comparing two page design options.

divided between two design options, the viewer does not have enough resources to handle the more complex processes involved in comparison (evaluating the characteristics of each, discerning the differences between them, forming an opinion based on two sets in visual input, etc.). Additionally, presenting two large page designs simultaneously necessitates scrolling on the part of the respondent, which further impedes the ability to retain any detail about what is presented. In short, testing two complex images—those containing multiple visual elements (e.g., web pages) or a high degree of visual detail (e.g., photographs)—simply puts too much demand on the participant to allow for a meaningful comparison within 5 s.

However, in the same way the method may be modified to test slogans and taglines, it can be viable for comparing *very simple* design elements, like logos or icons. Again, certain test safeguards need to be in place:

- The test instructions must specify that two options will be presented, and that a comparison will be required as part of the test: "You are about to view two options for a logo design. Compare the two as best you can before answering the questions." This will set the proper expectation and help prevent confusion when the options are presented.
- The test image must accommodate the two options in a single view, without requiring the participant to scroll. The options should be in close proximity to each other, so that minimal eye movements are required to move back and forth between them. Nonintrusive labels (e.g., "A" and "B") may be added in order to reference each option while answering the questions.
- Questions should be limited to the respondents' perception of the options or the emotional response(s) they elicit. These can be framed either as open questions or closed questions, but the researcher should be aware of the potential limitations of each. Open questions ("How do you describe the difference(s) between the logos?", "How does one logo compare to the other?") will encourage longer and potentially more robust responses, but with each question asked, responses may become less precise due to memory fade. Closed questions ("Which option best conveys the value of 'confidence'?", "Which logo do you prefer?") are easier for respondents to answer and will provide more easily quantifiable data, but could increase

the likelihood of habituation, a reflexive repetition of answers that will be discussed further in Section 2.6.

Predicting Future Behavior

It is not uncommon for a test to ask respondents to predict their future behavior, based on solely the image they viewed. Indeed, 16% of the tests analyzed for this book contained questions along the lines of "Would you hire this company?" or "Would you sign up for this service?" These were usually asked at the end of a question sequence, seemingly in an attempt to generate some sense of security for the business stakeholders—i.e., "if a certain percentage of people indicate that they would take some positive action based on our web site design, then our design decisions must be good ones." (One especially optimistic test actually asked: "Would you use this product if you saw successfully aggregated news and content at the top, *and* if the site was much better designed?")

Upon closer inspection, inquiries like these aren't really seeking to predict future behavior so much as to gauge perceived trust and/or credibility. At a subliminal level, the question "Would you hire this company?" really means "Is this company trustworthy?" Likewise, "Would you sign up for this service?" really means "Have we established enough credibility to make you buy what we're selling?" Five-second tests can be used to test a design for perceived trust and credibility (this will be discussed in far more detail in Chapter 4), but the first step in getting data toward that end is to recognize the difference between (a) a design that elicits a sense of trust in those that view it and (b) a design that will actually prompt a future action or behavior by those who view it. In the case of the latter, neither the five-second test nor any other nonpredictive UX or design research method is going to provide viable results.

Testing Home and Landing Pages

Finally, a few words should be said on the appropriateness of the method with respect to testing home or landing pages. Chapter 1 noted that the originators of the method discouraged its use for evaluating home page designs, instead limiting its scope to determining whether the purpose of a *content page* is obvious. From a functional standpoint, the main purposes of a home or landing page are generally universal: (a) to give users high-level information about a site and (b) to provide a means of getting to the more specific content areas within the site. Under the original method guidelines, responses received to the question "What is the purpose of this home page?" would be largely predetermined, and the point of testing for purpose becomes fairly meaningless, so the cautions of the method originators (Perfetti, 2013) were well founded.

However, Chapter 1 also noted that the online tool providers are positioning the method as being "ideal" for testing home or landing pages. Researchers appear to be willing to take the bait—nearly half of the tests analyzed for this book were focused on these types of pages. However, fewer than 10% of those tests contained questions directly relating to the page's function or purpose, indicating at least some degree of understanding on the part of those testing home pages that the method may have something to offer beyond what was originally intended.

Consider the example of an actual home page test, which asked the following three questions:

1. "What is the name of the company?"
2. "What does the company sell?"
3. "What do you recall most about the page?"

This test clearly does not speak to the page's purpose, but one could argue that these are perfectly reasonable questions to ask after five seconds' worth of exposure to a home or landing page design. Rather than explicitly emphasizing the page's purpose, this test represents a quest for useful data that may help guide other specific aspects of the page's visual design, such as:

• which elements of the page stand out in general memory;
• whether specific visual targets on the page are easily discerned or remembered;
• whether the design of a page elicits a specific emotional response;
• whether the design communicates values that the designer wishes to be represented.

A more detailed examination of specific test focuses and formats will be provided in Section 2.2. The central point here is that the five-second test can indeed be used for evaluating home pages *for certain types of data* unrelated to the purpose of the page.

Rule #1: Don't Use a Five-Second Test When a Different Research Method will Produce Better Results for You

- The five-second test is not a substitute for other types of research. Let the research question(s) guide whether it represents an appropriate option.
- The five-second test is the *wrong* choice for anything requiring more than five seconds' worth of exposure in order to provide a meaningful answer, including:
    - Reading and understanding text/copy (see **Reading text**)
    - Assessing more than one page design at a time (see **Comparing design options**)
    - Expected outcomes after viewing a design (see **Predicting future behavior**)
- Contrary to the original intent of the method, it can be used to test home or landing pages *for certain types of data* (see **Testing home and landing pages**)

2.2 TEST FORMAT

With the research questions established, the method options considered, and the decision reached that a five-second test is appropriate for the research, it's time to consider which test format is most appropriate. There are a number of different formats for five-second tests, each of which has its own set of guidelines, limitations, and opportunities for customization. Sometimes the need is for factual information about a specific facet within a design; other times there is a need to know what type of reaction a design elicits. The important point here is that knowing what you want to achieve—or, what you want the data to tell you—will help determine which format to use, keep the test focused, and assist in the crafting of the remaining test components. It will also help filter out unnecessary or irrelevant questions, which could frustrate or annoy your respondents, increase abandonment rates and/or nonresponse answers, and jeopardize your data.

Memory Dump Tests

The most basic of five-second tests, the "memory dump," is just that: an emptying of the respondents' short-term memory, resulting in a list of things remembered about a design. This test approach aligns almost exactly with the original intent of the method (as described in

Chapter 1) and can help confirm whether specific elements stand out in support of the business goals—or, conversely, it can help identify elements that need design attention. For instance, take the example of a company that wishes to reduce phone traffic for its call center by driving online users to their web site's chat function (Figure 2.3). If the results of a memory dump test show that people do not remember seeing a link to chat, but do remember seeing the support phone number and links to help articles, the design of the page may need to be reconsidered.

While the mechanics of this approach are the same when using online tools as they are when using the original "in-person" approach, there is a key difference in execution. Whereas participants in the lab are free to write down everything they remember, the online tools usually provide a finite number of individual response boxes (typically no more than five) in which respondents can enter their answers. The result is a list of items that is not as broad as it might be if respondents were free to note everything they can remember, but which does identify the "top things remembered" consistently by respondents. (Theoretically a single question can ask the user to note everything

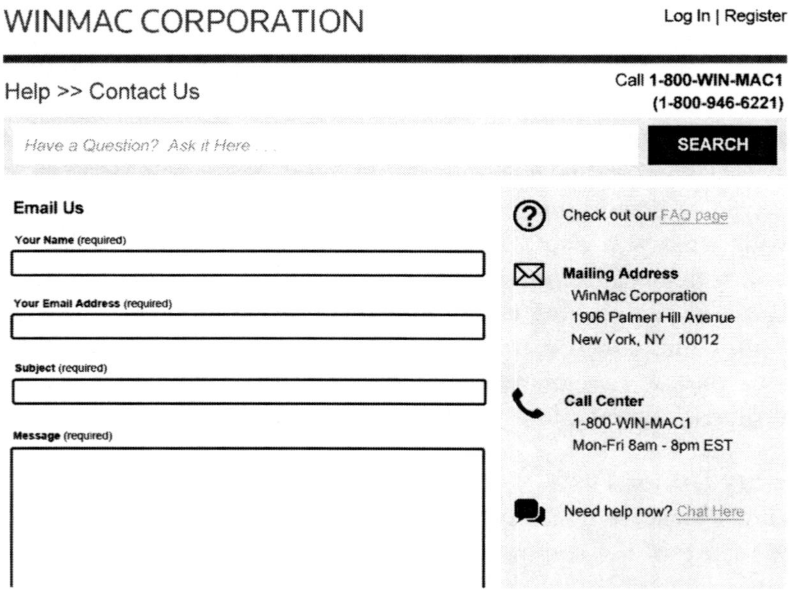

WINMAC CORPORATION   Log In | Register

Help >> Contact Us   Call **1-800-WIN-MAC1**
                                                         (1-800-946-6221)

Have a Question? Ask it Here . . .   **SEARCH**

Email Us   (?) Check out our FAQ page

Your Name (required)

                                      ✉   **Mailing Address**
                                           WinMac Corporation
Your Email Address (required)   1906 Palmer Hill Avenue
                                           New York, NY   10012

Subject (required)
                                      📞   **Call Center**
                                           1-800-WIN-MAC1
Message (required)   Mon-Fri 8am - 8pm EST

                                      💬   Need help now? Chat Here

Figure 2.3 "Contact Us" page example.

they remember in a single response box; however, due to character limitations and the fact that single line response boxes encourage shorter responses, this is neither practical nor recommended.)

As in all five-second tests, the "reverse Polaroid" effect is very much in play in memory dump tests. However, with no targeted questions guiding the responses (as in other test types), results can be expected to follow a specific pattern of specific-to-general. Using the current example of the online support page, the first two items reported will likely identify specific targets on a page, such as "the company name" or "the phone number in the upper right corner." As memory fade takes hold, subsequent responses will likely refer to general site attributes, such as "the clean, modern design" or "the layout of the Email Us form," and/or attitudinal comments such as "the page was too crowded—create some space so it's easier to read." (Section 2.6 will describe an experiment that illustrates this tendency in more detail.)

Since there are no questions eliciting specific types of feedback, many of the rules pertaining to the formulation of questions (number, order, wording, etc.) do not apply for memory dump tests. However, it is important that the test instructions set the proper expectation before the test image is shown—i.e., that participants should remember as much as they can about what they see, and that they will be asked to document the things they remember most vividly.

Target Identification Tests

This format focuses on specific "targets"—visual elements or information—in a design. Questions in this type of test aim to directly challenge a respondent's recall of one or more targets—unlike the memory dump, in which the obviousness of a specific target is gleaned through analysis of the test data. As a result, the researcher can learn not just whether a target is noticeable, but also whether specific aspects of that target are memorable. For the online support page example, possible questions in a target identification test might be:

- "Where was the phone number for contacting the call center located?"
- "Between what hours is phone support available?"
- "Where on the page was the link to the chat functionality?"

As noted in the memory dump test, respondents seem to have a natural tendency toward reporting specifics about a design first; however, the cognitive demands of recall and the effects of memory fade mean that the window for getting useful answers about specific targets is smaller than it is for other types of data. Consequently, the chances for getting useful results using this format are increased when the test is focused on a singular target. In addition, the individual test components—the instructions, number of questions, order of questions, etc. (all of which will be discussed further in this chapter)—are much more impactful to the outcome of target identification tests than in attitudinal or memory dump tests, so these tests must be designed with greater care.

Attitudinal Tests

This format focuses on what people like, believe, or perceive about a design. It is very much in line with traditional survey methodology, in that the data will reveal matters of opinion, such as aesthetic appeal, the emotional response, or degree of satisfaction that a design elicits, the degree to which a design conveys trustworthiness and/or credibility, and (harkening back to method's original intent) whether a page's purpose is perceived as being evident or obvious. For the online support page example, an attitudinal test might include questions such as:

- "What word(s) would you use to describe look and feel of the page you just saw?"
- "In your opinion, how well does the design emphasize the availability of chat to contact online support?"
- "Rate the overall visual appeal of the design on a scale of 1−10: 1 = 'not at all appealing,' 10: 'extremely appealing'. "

As with other types of surveys, care must be taken with respect to formation of instructions and questions, so as to minimize bias and the reporting of false data. However, this approach differs from most surveys in that the opinions are based on an immediate response to a specific visual, rather than stored knowledge about a product, service, behavior, or issue. The effects of memory fade are of course still in play, but are not as acute in this type of test—forming and expressing personal opinions about a design does not require as much recollection of design specifics, so the likelihood of nonresponses is comparatively low.

Mixed Tests

The vast majority of tests analyzed for this book used a "mixed" format—i.e., using components of more than one of the other test formats. By definition, this represents an "unfocused" approach that likely reflects either (a) a research goal that is not sufficiently specific or (b) a researcher that does not fully understand the limitations of the method. For our online support group example, a mixed test could look like this:

- "List one or two specific things you remember most about the page you just saw." (*from the memory dump test*)
- "What word(s) would you use to describe look and feel of the page you just saw?" (*from the attitudinal test*)
- "Where on the page was the link to the chat functionality?" (*from the target identification test*)

Results yielded in a mixed test are likely to be—well, mixed. This is not to say definitively that a mixed test will provide suboptimal data, but it does mean that the test needs to be constructed with careful attention to the other rules outlined in this chapter. For instance, the potential impact of question order can be illustrated in the test described above. If the memory of a design is sharpest when the first question is asked, it makes sense to ask target questions first. In the mixed test described here, by the time the respondent gets to the question about the location of the chat link, (s)he is less capable of recalling specifics about the design, thereby increasing the likelihood of a nonresponse. Some degree of useful data can be expected from the mixed test format, especially for the first one to two questions (followed by some likely drop-off as more questions are added). However, in keeping with good research practice, better results will be obtained by creating separate tests for each individual question.

Rule #2: Focus on the Specific Design Aspect(s) You Want to Test and Employ the Appropriate Test Format

- The **memory dump** test is most faithful to the original intent of the method and will indicate *what is most remembered* about a design.
- The **target identification** test uses direct questioning about *visual targets within a design* to gauge whether specific information about them is retained.

- The **attitudinal test** solicits opinions about the *perceived appeal, quality, and/or usefulness* of a design or any of its individual elements.
- It is more difficult, but not impossible, to obtain usable data from a **"mixed" test** that combines aspects of the other three types of tests.

2.3 AVOIDING THE NONRESPONSE

The main selling point of the five-second test method, and of using online tools to facilitate it, is that you can get specific feedback about a design quickly and fairly effortlessly. It is therefore very dispiriting to receive the results of a test and see multiple instances of empty or "I don't know" responses. (Experience has shown that in crowdsourced tests, respondents are more than willing to communicate the "I don't know" response in more creative ways.) Design and user experience research can be difficult to justify from a time and resource standpoint—results like this undercut the research effort and make the job much more difficult. It is therefore critical that precautionary actions be taken to minimize the likelihood of "empty data," so that the researcher has not wasted his/her time.

For our purposes, the "pass" and "I don't know" answers are considered to be forms of **nonresponse**—i.e., an instance where the required information is not obtained from a potential respondent. This differs somewhat from the definition commonly used in survey research, which specifies the absence of representation in a sample due to factors beyond the control of the researcher (Fowler, 2002)—e.g., the inability to contact potential respondents; the inability to persuade respondents to cooperate in a survey; and/or "not-able" factors, such as illness or language barriers. Regardless of any differences in definition, the two share the major negative consequence: unusable responses that reduce sample size, introduce the possibility of bias into the results, and/or result in wasted time, effort, and resources.

At first glance, five-second tests would appear to be insulated from many of the "factors beyond the control of the researcher" noted in the definition. For example, they presume a captive audience motivated in some way to provide feedback: in lab tests, participants have been specifically recruited (and likely compensated) for their participation, while participants in crowdsourced tests have likely come to an online testing site with the possibility of compensation, or to "do a good deed" for a fellow researcher in need of data. In either case, by the time the test is administered, contact has been made successfully, some level cooperation has been secured, and "not able" factors have been overcome. (In fact, the far more likely possibility in a crowd-sourced five-second test is a lazy, frustrated, and/or disinterested participant using a nonresponse as an easy means of moving on to something else).

Five-second tests are also very likely to be free of any emotional factors that could contribute to nonparticipation. In traditional surveys, emotional influence on responses is a reason why the inclusion of nonresponse options is considered—they allow respondents to indicate that they have not given any substantive thought to a particular issue, do not wish to give their opinions about a controversial subject, or do not have enough factual knowledge about a given topic to answer in an informed way. Conversely, participants in five-second tests are focused on an impersonal experience, based exclusively on the reaction to a common visual stimulus, and thus are not likely to activate emotional triggers that might cause hesitation.

The main issues seen in five-second tests lie not in the uncontrollable factors, but rather in research approaches and test structures that encourage nonresponses. As an example, one of the tests analyzed for this book involved the home page for an online retail outlet selling quinceneara dresses (Figure 2.4).

Included among the test questions was: "What is the quality of the dresses sold here?" At a micro level, this question has several things going against it—not the least of which are ineffective wording, referencing a test image that lacks examples upon which to form a basis of opinion, and the fact that it was included in a mixed test format. At a macro level, the problem is that the nature of the question almost guarantees a nonresponse. Conceptually, commenting on the quality of a dress would require some level of interaction with the garment itself—it needs to be held, examined, worn, and "experienced." It is simply not reasonable to ask a person to render an opinion on item quality based on a visual exposure to the home page of a web site—and certainly not when that exposure is limited to a mere 5 s. By asking such a question, the researcher has wasted much of what limited opportunity exists for getting meaningful feedback.

Figure 2.4 Quinceneara retail web site.

The quinceneara test is a somewhat egregious example of ensuring wasted time and effort by not giving enough thought to the test. In most cases, the risk of getting nonresponses can be tied to the type of test you choose to run. For instance,

- "In a memory dump test (in which respondents are simply listing as many things as they can remember about what they saw), it's virtually impossible to get an "I don't know" answer—everyone is likely to remember and report *something* about what they saw. The number of items remembered will vary from person to person, and the likelihood of a nonresponse will increase with each response requested, but you'll rarely, if ever, get a completely "empty" set of answers."
- "Likewise, people are very rarely without an opinion or attitude about how a design makes them feel or react, so attitudinal tests inherently discourage the nonresponse."
- "Tests that ask for factual data about a design are trickier—given the limitations of a five-second exposure, a respondent might legitimately not know where on a screen a specific button was located, or remember the words of a web site tagline or marketing slogan. The factors impacting the ability to test for factual data using this method are many and will be studied further in subsequent sections in this chapter."

To a certain degree—especially in online unmoderated tests—the data delivery mechanism can also impact the likelihood of non-responses. In online surveys, the risk can be mitigated somewhat by using response constructs that employ radio buttons or checkboxes instead of text-entry boxes. Another possibility is to not include non-response options but require that the question be answered before proceeding—however, this approach increases the risk of a participant providing "junk data" just to get out of the survey. In the current crop of five-second test tools, the only option for submitting an answer is to enter text in a box, meaning that the possibility of the "I don't know" or "I can't recall" response cannot be eliminated.

The easiest way to minimize the likelihood of the nonresponse—and this is a theme that this book will revisit often—is to continually refine the questions before formally launching the test. Pilot testing with friends, colleagues, and associates will help indicate the relative risk of nonresponse and (together with the rest of the rules) help identify any corrective actions to take before the formal launch. Keeping this rule firmly in mind from the start can not only help ensure useful data but can also help stretch the limits of what can be done with the method, as we'll see in more detail later on.

Rule #3: Don't Give Participants Any Excuse to Say "I Don't Know" or "I Don't Remember"

- Nonresponses represent wasted time, effort, and resources on the part of the researcher.
- Nonresponses in five-second tests are usually the result of controllable factors, such as test planning and structure.
- Different test formats carry different risk levels for getting nonresponses; memory dump tests carry the least risk, while target identification and mixed tests carry the greatest risk.
- When in doubt, conduct a few pilot tests to determine whether any questions present a high risk of getting nonresponses.

2.4 INSTRUCTIONS

Generally speaking, instructions serve two basic purposes:

1. To facilitate the completion of specific tasks
2. To provide necessary information relevant to the completion of a task

Writing proper instructions for five-second tests is very much a balancing act. You don't want to give away the questions that you're going to be asking, but you also want to give participants enough reasonable expectation so they provide the kind of data you're looking for. Instructions that are too general will not encourage the retention of specifics, which is important for certain test formats; on the other hand, instructions that are too specific will jeopardize the ability to provide feedback on the "big picture" of a design, which is important for other test formats.

Writing the Instructions

Recalling the original structure of the test as applied in the lab environment (see Section 1.2), readying participants for a five-second test involves a moderator employing a two-step process. First, preparatory instructions establish the test context by communicating the reasons why the research is being conducted. Second, test instructions inform participants of the test procedure—i.e., that an image will be displayed for 5 s, and that (s)he should try to remember as much as possible of what is displayed. In the age of unmoderated testing, there is no moderator to explain the test protocols and answer questions if the participant requires additional explanation. It is therefore incumbent upon the researcher to ensure that the instructions strike the proper balance of brevity and detail, reduce the likelihood of response bias, and adequately "set the table" for the participant to provide useful feedback.

At this point, a distinction needs to be made between two types of instructions that exist when using unmoderated test tools. The *preparatory instructions* are provided upon launch of the test tool and typically describe the tool and how it will be used—these are not unique to any single test, are typically hardcoded into the tool UI, and usually cannot be altered. The focus of this section will be on the writing of the *test instructions*, which include any necessary information the participant requires before viewing the test image. These are unique to each test and are the sole domain of the researcher or test planner, who (regardless of whether the test is moderated or unmoderated) is responsible for making sure that the test instructions are:

- **Clear:** Each sentence should represent a single concept or idea. Words should be chosen carefully and tested repeatedly, so that they are understood the same way by all who read them.

- **Concise:** Instructions cannot be perceived as lengthy. In most cases, instructions should be limited to only one or two short sentences.
- **Sufficient:** Instructions should establish realistic expectation(s) about what is going to be presented (Redish, 2012). It's sometimes advantageous to create specific contexts in order to set expectations; however, proper instructions refrain from presenting unnecessary or unrealistic contexts (more on this topic later in this section).
- **Appropriate for the test format:** Section 2.2 noted that the format is important in ensuring that the data is appropriate and useful. Proper instructions indicate the format in such a way that participants will understand what types of data they will be asked to provide.

Considerations by Test Format

Recall that the goal of the **memory dump test** is to determine which elements stand out in a design. Since this format does not include questions that reference specific elements or delve into participant opinions about them, the instructions need not go beyond what the method originators used—a simple statement about the process that is to occur. (This is also the best strategy for **mixed tests**.) Possible variations include:

- "You will have 5 s to view the image. Afterward, you'll be asked a few short questions."
- "You'll see a screen for a few seconds—try to remember as much as you can about what you see."
- "After viewing a design for 5 s, be prepared to tell us what you recall about it."

Note the wording of the calls to action in these examples. They are reflective of a trend mentioned previously: namely, those respondents tend to focus on and report specific design elements first. Instructions that prompt the participant to "remember as much as you can" or to "let us know what parts jumped out at you" will virtually guarantee that specific elements—logos, messages, buttons, colors, etc.—will be reported as the "things remembered." This approach will not work for **attitudinal tests**, which contain opinion-centered questions that require the participant to recall, consider and comment on the design as a whole entity. For this test format, setting the correct expectation in the instructions means putting the participant in the proper frame of mind for delivering opinion-based responses. A slight alteration to the memory dump instructions is one way to accomplish this:

- "You will have 5 s to view the image. Afterward, you'll be asked a few short questions about your general reaction to the design."
- "You'll see a screen for a few seconds—pay attention to the general aesthetic and visual appeal of the design."
- "After viewing a design for 5 s, we'll ask for your opinions on its look and feel."

Instructions are a little trickier in **target identification tests**, because the focus is on the participant's ability to comment on one or more specific elements. Most research methods warn strongly against wording tasks or questions in ways that lead the participants to the answers, in order to see if participants can find the answer(s) themselves (and to help prevent biased or unrealistic data). However, because this particular method requires that the design be removed from view after 5 s, sometimes it's necessary to reference the target in the instructions, so that the participant has enough time to view and consider it. If, for example, a target ID test contains questions solely about a web site's navigation bar, it is probably better to reference the bar in the instructions, so that the participant will seek out and focus attention on the bar for the full 5 s. On the other hand, if you want to know whether a design facilitates finding a specific target instantly, it's better to not reference it in the instructions. To reiterate an earlier point, it's all about the research goal(s) and knowing what you want to learn.

"Imagining" the Context

In addition to setting expectations and facilitating the completion of tasks, good instructions intend to put participants at ease prior to the actual test launch, the better to receive useful data. A common way of doing this in five-second tests is to ask participants to put themselves in a specific context, usually by using the words "imagine" or "pretend" (24% of the tests analyzed for this book featured instructions that did so). When used properly, context statements can add realistic "color" to the instructions and ground participants in a situation of relative familiarity. Consider the instructions for a test about the design of a poster ad: "Imagine that you are standing on the street and a bus drives past. You see an advertisement on the back." This is a fairly effective use of a context statement—pretty much anybody can relate to this scenario, and its inclusion may assist in putting the respondent in a better frame of mind to answer the subsequent test questions.

However, this strategy becomes a problem when instructions include unnecessary or unrealistic contexts:

- An *unnecessary context* adds no value or practical assistance to the participant's ability to answer the test questions, regardless of the format used. For example, actual tests have included instructions such as "Imagine that you are looking at the following page" and "Imagine you found this site using a search engine."
- An *unrealistic context* occurs when a participant is asked to imagine a situation to which (s)he cannot relate, thereby risking participant hostility or indifference to the test. The chances of this happening are greatest when the participant population has not been recruited against a specific persona or profile, as in crowdsourced testing. Consider this example: "Imagine that you're researching software vendors for your bank." If the test's participants consist solely of bank employees or software purchasers, this context statement has some validity. In a crowdsourced test, however, the likelihood of the sample containing bank employees or software purchasers is likely to be low, placing most participants into a situation to which they will have trouble relating.

Context statements need not be universally accessible in order to be useful, but they rarely work well as instructions in and of themselves. Note that most of the "imagine" examples above contain no indication of the test format—they simply place participants in a context without any indication of what kinds of responses will be asked of them. Supplementing a context statement with an indication of test format can help alleviate any potential negative impact of an unrealistic context. "Imagine that you're researching software vendors for your bank" becomes more accessible (and less easily dismissed) when combined with "You'll be asked for your opinion about the web site's color scheme."

Rule #4: Devote Time to Crafting Proper Instructions

- Instructions should be clear, concise, sufficient, and appropriate for the test format (see **Writing the instructions**).

- Instructions can be kept general for memory dump and mixed format tests. Attitudinal and target identification tests may require more specificity (see **Considerations by test format**).
- When using context statements, supplement them with test format indicators. Avoid the use of unnecessary or unrealistic contexts (see **"Imagining" the context**).

2.5 PAGE/IMAGE VISIBILITY

Imagine being asked to give your opinion on a book after reading only the first sentence, or to rate a movie based solely on the opening credits, or to describe Van Gogh's "Starry Night" after only a glimpse at the painting's top left corner. Exercises in futility, to say the least—yet that is exactly what played out in nearly half of the tests analyzed for this book. Unfortunately, examples such as that shown in Figure 2.5 are all too typical in five-second tests.

The instructions for this test asked participants to compare four logo variations, to consider that the logo options are intended to represent a web development business, and to remember each logo's assigned number when answering the three test questions. Think about the sequence of events that plays out in this test:

1. The test image is presented, and the participant gets grounded in the initial view, taking in that which is visible.
2. The participant realizes that scrolling will be required to view the rest of the image.

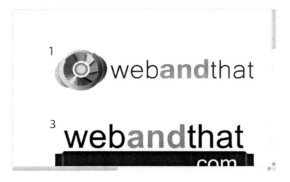

Figure 2.5 Logo comparison test using a very large image.

3. The participant homes in on the vertical scrolling mechanism, moves the mouse, clicks and holds the mouse button, and preforms the scroll.
4. The participant gets grounded in the new view, taking in that which is visible.
5. The participant realizes that more scrolling will be required to view the rest of the image.
6. Step 3 is repeated as needed for horizontal scrolling.

Having spent the better part of the allotted 5 s manipulating the screen, the participant is then asked to answer the following questions:

Q1. "Which logo did you like most?"
Q2. "Which logo had the best design?"
Q3. "Do any of the logos remind you of web development?"

This test example has a number of big deficiencies, but the most egregious by far is the burden placed on the participant to simply view the logo options under consideration. A person cannot comment meaningfully on that which cannot be seen or is made too difficult to see. Any interference in a participant's ability to view a test image in its totality greatly increases the likelihood of getting nonresponses to test questions, even in a test as basic as a memory dump.

Does Scrolling Influence Ability to Recall a Target?
While image scrolling has a negative impact in all test formats, the greatest effect is in target identification tests and in mixed format tests that include target identification questions. In most instances (or unless prompted otherwise), participants are inclined to internalize specific elements first. The process of scrolling an image inhibits this inclination.

However, one could argue that as long as the test target(s) are visible before scrolling is necessary, it shouldn't matter whether a large image is used or not. To test this argument, the author conducted a set of tests to see whether the likelihood of nonresponse answers increases when using a large image that requires scrolling. Two separate tests were performed using product pages from the web site of a toy distributor, each with a different brand/product highlighted on the page (Figure 2.6). In each test, participants were given the same standard instructions: "You are about to see a page from the web site of a product distributor. You will be asked one question about what you see." After viewing the page for 5 s, the question was asked: "What is the

Figure 2.6 Image size for Test B: page is cropped at the bottom.

specific brand highlighted on the page?" In both tests, the target brand information was visible in the view when the image was presented. However, in Test A, the full page was presented at 960×2914, such that vertical scrolling would be accommodated in the test window (even if the participant didn't use it). In Test B, the page was cropped at the bottom, eliminating the possibility of scrolling.

(For the purposes of this experiment, it did not matter whether the participant identified the corporate parent company or the individual toy brand as the "specific brand" highlighted; remember, the focus of the test was on whether there was any difference in the number of nonresponses.)

The results (Figure 2.7) indicate that large images that require scrolling do in fact increase the likelihood of nonresponses. In Test A, 5 of 21 answers were nonresponses. Because these were unmoderated tests, there is no way of knowing whether there were outside influences or distractions in play, but it makes sense that at least some participants spent valuable time scrolling the page, at the expense of discerning or retaining any specific visual elements. In Test B, with the image fully visible and the possibility of scrolling is removed, only 2 of 21 answers were nonresponses. This is indicative of a group of participants able to devote full attention to the totality of the image without the temptation of scrolling.

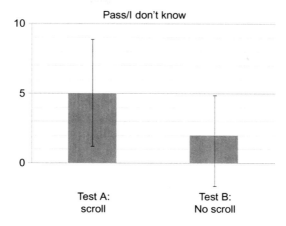

Figure 2.7 Image size test results, n = 21 for each test (95% confidence level).

Creating the Test Image

The lack of control inherent in unmoderated testing means that the researcher has to be thoughtful about how the image is presented within the test. Consideration must be given not only to the design that will be presented but also to the technologies (especially screen resolutions) used by the likely testers. If, for example, you are creating a crowdsourced test, and you know that more than half of the world's computer users are using resolutions larger than 1024×768, providing a test image at those dimensions will be nonscrollable for a significant portion of your respondents. (Doing an Internet search on "browser display statistics" should provide a number of current resources to reference as you consider the technologies of who might be taking your tests.) Ultimately, however, it is the responsibility of the researcher to ensure that the image used in the test eliminates (or at least keeps to an absolute minimum) the effects of scrolling.

For in-person lab testing, it's a simple matter of knowing what monitor will display the test image and customizing the image to fit the screen resolution. In the case of unmoderated tests, most of the online tool providers offer two ways of submitting the test image. Firstly, a web page URL can be entered into a box, and the tool will automatically create a screen capture of the entire page; however, this approach will not scale the page down to fit within a single view (even if it did, there would likely be a quality degradation that would make the image unsuitable for test purposes). Alternatively, a precreated image (usually in jpg, .png, or .gif format) can be uploaded to the tool. This option gives the researcher far greater control over scrolling, but usually requires that some resizing take place before uploading. Cropping and scaling are the two most common ways of resizing images; each should be considered carefully for the potentially negative impacts on how test images are presented and, thus, the likelihood of nonresponses:

- **Cropping** (as used in the toy brand experiment outlined in this section) will preserve the image detail necessary to provide a realistic view of the design but provides only a segment of the image at the cost of losing the context of the image as a whole.
- **Scaling** will retain the entirety of the image but could degrade the image detail so much that the image becomes too distracting to elicit meaningful feedback. (If one or the other does not suffice, combining the techniques may provide an acceptable balance of preserving context and presenting discernible detail.)

If resizing is required, be mindful of the instructions and test questions before deciding which method to use. For example, if the image is cropped, the instructions should specify to participants that only a portion of the entire page or design is being displayed. In this way, the participant is less likely to be confused when the image is presented, and more attention can be paid to what is visible, rather than wondering what is missing. The main concern is to make sure that the participant is put in the best position possible to meaningful feedback about the design.

Rule #5: Optimize the Test Image so that Scrolling is Eliminated

- Use images that do not force the viewer to scroll, yet provide the visual information necessary for participants to answer test questions meaningfully.
- Forcing participants to scroll an image means less time for them to internalize the design you want to test and increases the likelihood of "I don't know" responses (see **Does scrolling influence ability to recall a target?**).
- If necessary, use cropping and/or scaling to make the test image fit the test window (see **Creating the test image**).

2.6 NUMBER OF QUESTIONS

Best practices touted by the leading online survey tool providers (Johnson, 2012; McKee, 2013) consistently state that surveys are most effective when they are short, clear, and to the point. SurveyMonkey further reports that participants of their online surveys require no more than 5 min for the average participant to complete, and that this can be achieved with about 10 questions (Chudoba, 2011). Five-second tests would appear, then, to have a lot of built-in advantages as a means of getting a lot of usable data quickly. If that were indeed the case, we would not need to pay so much attention to minimizing non-responses to test questions. To be sure, there are a number of interrelated factors that need to be examined (and will be in subsequent sections of this chapter), but the number of questions asked is indeed a factor that needs to be considered.

In keeping with their narrow research goals, the original test requirements of Perfetti et al. (see Chapter 1) contained two information requests:

1. Recall as much as you can remember about the design.
2. What is the purpose of the page?

The researchers understood that there's a limit to the amount of information one can reasonably expect from a test participant after only 5 s of exposure to a design. However, this lesson appears to have been lost (or was never really learned) by those who use the online testing tools of today. Of the tests analyzed for this book, 80% contained three or more questions, with the largest percentage by far (37%) containing five questions, the maximum number usually provided by the UsabilityHub tool.

Which is not to say that a test consisting of five questions is inherently less effective than a test consisting of two questions—that would be an unfair generalization. The thing to remember is that this type of test puts into play specific memory dynamics that impact how many questions can or should be asked. Test participants don't want to feel their time is being wasted, they don't want to be confused, and they don't want to roll their eyes in disbelief thinking, "Are you really asking me that?" Being brief, clear, and to the point means understanding how much information the participant is reasonably capable of providing, and asking the minimum number of questions required to extract that information.

The Ticking Clock

As noted in Chapter 1, the number of things a person can memorize and recall at any given time is a subject of ongoing debate. In one of the most frequently cited papers in psychological research, Miller (1956) put the "magic number" at seven, plus or minus two. (Obviously some people can memorize more, others less, but seven appeared to be where most of the "magic" happened.) Subsequent research has put the number as high as ten and as low as four. For our purposes, the exact number is irrelevant—the points that need to be made are (a) that the brain cannot retain very much new information in the short term and (b) that the cognitive tasks involved in completing a five-second test will have an eroding effect on what is memorized.

Recall what occurs during the "reverse Polaroid" effect: once an image is removed from view, the perceptual processes cease, putting a larger burden on the memory processes. In five-second tests, the acts of reading, understanding, and responding to questions place additional burden on the cognitive processes in play, which contribute further to memory fade. It follows that for each question asked in a test, the increased cognitive load reduces the amount of working memory that the participant has to comprehend and respond to those questions, lessening his/her ability to answer them with precision. This "ticking clock" is in place regardless of the test format; however, it is more pronounced in target identification and in mixed tests that contain target identification questions, so the number of questions in these formats should be kept as low as possible.

Can the Number of Questions in a Test Predict What Types of Answers Are Received?

Some degree of memory drop-off has to be expected for most participants as a test precondition. The question then is how much specificity can a researcher expect over the course of a test containing five questions (the usual maximum in a five-second test)? The author devised an experiment to determine whether the types of answers given could be predicted, using the front page of a tourism site for a major US city as the subject. Participants were instructed to view the page and be prepared to name five things they remembered about it (this is very much in line with the original intent of the testing model of Perfetti et al.). After viewing the page, participants were asked:

- **Q1.** "What is the first thing you remember about the design?"
- **Q2.** "What is the second thing you remember about the design?," etc.

It was expected that the responses would get increasingly abstract with each question asked, and that at some point, the likelihood of getting a usable answer would be low.

The results (Figure 2.8) show that participants overwhelmingly responded to the first two "things remembered" questions with a specified or implied visual target—usually the name of the city or the slogan for Q1, followed by a reference to a specific photo or a call to action ("get a free booklet," "book travel online," etc.) for Q2. Starting at Q3, the precision of the responses begins to change rapidly, shifting more toward references to look and feel and other general site attributes ("the color scheme," "web 1.0 looking," "Lots of text I didn't read," etc.). By Q4, about half of all respondents did not provide an answer with any specificity, electing instead to either pass on the questions or explicitly state "nothing" or "I don't remember."

To further gauge the specific-to-general trend, the test was replicated using the tourism site of a different city. Results (Figure 2.9) showed trends that were highly similar to those seen in the first test.

In fact, the combined results of the two tests produced only one respondent who referenced a specific or implied target in all five responses.

It is notable that in both tests, controls were put in place to minimize memory fade—the instructions set the expectation up-front that recall was going to be required, and the wording of the questions was repetitive to minimize the cognitive processing needed to access that recall. Nonetheless, the results indicate that, even in an exercise as "abbreviated" as a five-second test, there is a point at which users will stop giving useful data.

Is There a "Magic Number" of Questions?
Five-second tests are by and large "self-limiting"—i.e., given the nature of the tests themselves, the practicality of asking only a few questions is

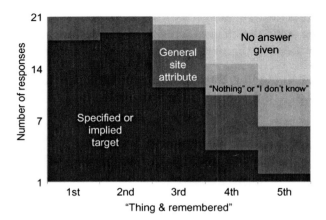

Figure 2.8 Declining trends for answer specificity, Test 1; n = 21.

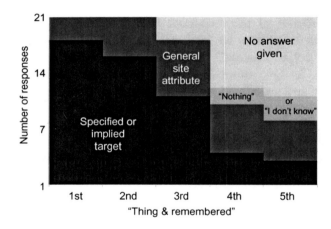

Figure 2.9 Declining trends for answer specificity, Test 2; n = 21.

fairly self-evident. Additionally, most online testing tools allow no more than five questions per test. So for anyone insisting on a magic number, it is almost certainly as few as possible, but "no more than five."

In truth, the real answer depends—as it so often does in UX or design research—on how focused the test is, and what responses can be expected given the realities of working memory and the impact of memory fade on it. If the purpose of a test is focused on the memorability of general design attributes, up to five questions can be asked with reasonable confidence that (a) the test will be completed with usable answers and (b) the instances of nonanswers will be low. Likewise, if the test is focused on getting attitudinal data, up to five questions can be asked with reasonable confidence. Tests highly focused on the memorability of details or the identification of specific targets should be limited to only two or three questions per test. If more than three questions are used, factors such as question order will increase in importance.

There is an additional potential benefit to reducing the number of questions in a target identification test. Any remaining available response mechanisms can be used to get data unrelated to the targets, such as emotional response data (how the participant felt about the design) or demographic data, which can be very useful in crowd-sourced tests or tests where the participant pool has not been screened against a persona or profile.

Rule #6: There is No "Magic Number" for How Many Questions to Ask, But Fewer are Usually Better

- Working memory is finite and temporary. Be respectful of how much your participants can reasonably retain in 5 s. The act of reading, considering, and answering questions can reduce the participant's ability to answer them, so ask as few as is necessary to get the information you need (see **The Ticking Clock**).
- Expect test responses to have a steady decline in specificity after the first two questions (see **Can the number of questions in a test predict what types of answers are received?**).
- The memory dump and attitudinal formats do not require special attention to specific design elements, so useful responses can be expected for up to five questions. For the target identification and mixed formats, which likely require attention to specific design elements, limit the number of questions to two or three (see **Is there a "magic number" of questions?**).

2.7 ORDER OF QUESTIONS

If using fewer questions is usually better, it might be assumed that the order in which those questions are presented is not very important. On the contrary, research has shown that disregarding the order in which information is structured and presented in surveys, questionnaires, and interviews can have significant impact on the responses received

(Brace, 2013), and five-second tests are not immune. Suboptimal question order was identified as a "violation" in 38% of the tests analyzed for this book, even in cases when the test contained only two questions.

It is beyond the scope of this book to summarize the large body of research regarding question ordering (e.g., McFarland, 1981; Bradburn and Mason, 1964; Boyle et al., 1993). Rather, researchers using the five-second test would do well to be reminded of a few of the cornerstone guidelines, how they apply to five-second tests, and how the unique characteristics of the method raise additional issues related to question order.

Priming and Habituation

Priming occurs when the answer to any question is influenced by a prior question (Brace, 2013). Mentioning something in one question can make people think of it while they answer a later question, when they might not have thought of it if it had not been previously mentioned. Section 2.4 noted the risk of this bias occurring with instructions that "tip off" the participant, but this can occur between questions as well, even when the test contains only two questions. Researchers need to be aware of the influence that prior questions can have in their five-second tests, write their tests accordingly, and interpret the responses with an eye on the possible effects.

Habituation (*How Habituation Can Negatively Affect Your Survey Reponses*, 2011) occurs when respondents give the same answer, or very similar answers, repeatedly in a series of questions, out of laziness, disinterest, or simply without really considering it. For example, consider a survey participant that is asked to assign a 1−10 rating to a very long list of options. (S)he may give more forthright and considerate answers early on, but put forth less effort as fatigue sets in and the dynamic of assigning a rating becomes repetitive. For the five-second tester, this might not appear to be a concern, as the inherently limited number of questions makes it less likely that fatigue or disinterest would be allowed to take hold. However, especially with crowdsourced tests, motivation for active engagement and thoughtful consideration as questions are answered could be very low. Researchers need to be aware of the potential impacts on responses and monitor the questions they ask, so that the participants remain engaged and involved in the test.

Memory Fade and Test Format

Interviews and surveys typically begin with the more general questions relating to the topic, before working through to the more specific or detailed subject matter (Brace, 2013). This practice establishes rapport and comfort level with the participant, and also grounds him/her in the dynamics of the method. However, participants in this type of research scenario are typically giving answers about a topic or issue about which they have prior knowledge, or about previous experience taking place more than a few minutes prior to the survey—in other words, experiences that leverage long-term memory in order to recall and respond.

As we've seen, five-second tests work almost entirely within the realm of short-term memory. Only a very limited number of details about the displayed design are likely to be retained in 5 s, and researchers would do well to consider how question order can help leverage that limited retention before it starts to fade. Consider this very simple two-question test example:

Q1. "What are one or two words you would use to describe the look and feel of the site?"
Q2. "What words or phrases do you remember from the web site?"

Since people tend to think more when asked the earlier questions in a series and thus give more accurate answers to them, it makes sense that the best chance of getting accurate answers to factual questions (Q2) would be achieved by asking it first in the sequence. (Reversing the order may also reduce the risk of receiving nonresponses and lessen the likelihood of priming effects). However, there is an argument for keeping the recall question as Q2: with the participant having used up some short-term memory resources providing a response for Q1, whatever words or phrases are remembered for Q2 are truly memorable.

Another consideration is the test format (see Rule #2). In a mixed test, the likelihood of nonresponses is reduced when target questions, which require more short-term memory resources, are grouped together and asked before attitudinal questions. Consider this mixed test example from the corpus of tests analyzed for this book:

Q1. "What was the name of the company who owns this site?"
Q2. "What was most prominent when you first viewed the page?"

Q3. "What did you like most about the design?"

Q4. "What was most off-putting about the design of this web site?"

Q5. "Can you name some of the products this company appears to sell?"

Leaving aside the potential priming effects Q1 may have on Q2, notice how the test starts with a target identification question, then proceeds with three perceptual or attitudinal/opinion questions before returning to a final target question. By asking for recall of the company's products last, memory fade makes the likelihood of getting an "I don't know" or "I can't remember" response much greater. A more optimal order for reducing the number of nonanswers would be:

Q1. "What was the name of the company who owns this site?"

Q2. "Can you name some of the products this company appears to sell?"

Q3. "What was most prominent when you first viewed the page?"

Q4. "What did you like most about the design?"

Q5. "What was most off-putting about the design of this web site?"

Does Question Order Impact the Ability to Recall Specific Targets?

Even when a test does not use a mixed format, question order should be looked at carefully. As previously noted, target identification questions place the most demand on a participant's short-term memory, and as a result, the impact on someone's ability to recall details through even a small sequence of questions is acute. Memory fade takes over, even when the test sets the expectation up-front that target recall is going to be required.

The author devised an experiment to test the concept that the ability to recall a specific visual element is impacted by the position of the recall question in the test. For this experiment, the same basic page layout (Figure 2.10) was modified for use in three different tests.

While the site name, product focus, color scheme, and text content were changed in each test instance, the design template remained the same. Because the test populations were crowdsourced using the UsabilityHub.com karma points feature, there were no controls in

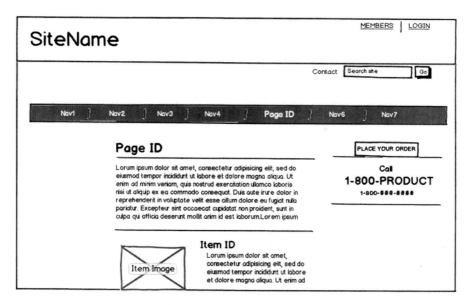

Figure 2.10 Wireframe of page design used in three tests.

place for keeping a participant from taking part in both tests. For this reason, changing the visual details within a consistent design template was considered adequate for illustrating the point (admittedly, using the same design but changing the order would have been a more optimal research approach).

The instructions were designed to set an expectation up-front that the participant would be asked to remember specific visual targets in the design: "After viewing the webpage, you will be asked to identify specific things about it." Finally, the same five questions were asked in each test:

1. "What is the name of the site?" (target = SiteName)
2. "What specific page of the overall site was shown?" (target = pageID)
3. "What is the item highlighted for sale on the page?" (target = itemID)
4. "How would someone place an order?" (target = call 1-800-product)
5. "Please briefly state the mission or purpose of the site." (nontarget question)

The research focus was on the question about the SiteName target— because of the larger text size and the prominent location in the upper left corner, this visual element was assumed to be the most easily perceived and remembered within a five-second span. The position of the site name question in the sequence was expected to influence the number of correct responses per test:

- In Test A, it was asked as the first question in the sequence (as shown above). The expectation was that the number of correct responses would be high, and that the number of nonresponses would be low.
- In Test B, the order of the four target questions was reversed, with the "SiteName" question moving to fourth in the sequence. The expectation was that memory fade would cause the number of correct responses to decrease, with the number of nonresponses increasing.
- In Test C, the reversed order of the questions was retained, but the nontarget "mission/purpose" question was moved to third in the sequence. The expectation was that the insertion of a "distracter" question in the middle of the test would cause the number of correct responses to the "SiteName" question to be even lower than in Test B.

The expectations were validated by the results (Figure 2.11). When recall of the site name was asked as the first question (Test A), 16 of 22 respondents correctly identified the site name. When asked as the fourth question (Test B), it went down to 8 of 22. The addition of the

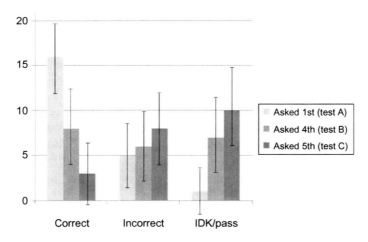

Figure 2.11 Results for recall of the "SiteName" target. n = 22 for Test A, n = 21 for Tests B and C (95% confidence level).

distractor question (Test C) lowered the number to 3 of 22. At the same time, the instances of "pass" and "I don't know/remember" went up just as steadily: when the site name question was asked first (Test A), only one respondent provided a nonresponse; when asked as the last question (Test C), 10 did so.

It is notable that upon reviewing the data for the "1-800-product" target question, the ordering effect was confirmed in the numbers of both correct responses and nonresponses (Figure 2.12). When asked as the first question (Test B), 10 of 21 respondents correctly referenced the 1-800 number information, with 5 passing or saying "I don't know." When asked as the second question (in Test C), only 5 answered correctly, with 10 providing a nonresponse. When asked as the fourth question (in Test A), the results were 4 of 22 correct and 12 of 22 nonresponses.

These results underscore the caution the researcher must use when reporting test results. For example, executive managers who value brand retention above all else would be encouraged by the results of Test A (16 of 22 correctly identified the site name) but discouraged by the results of Test C (3 of 21). Likewise, sales managers who want to be sure the means of placing an order is prominent and memorable would likely panic after hearing the results of Test A (4 of 22 correct) but might be optimistic with the results of Test B (10 of 21 correct).

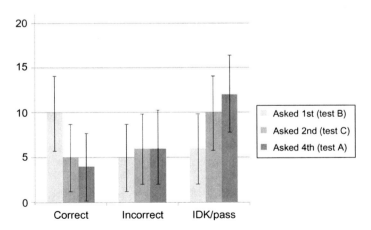

Figure 2.12 Results for recall of the "1-800-product" target. n = 22 *for Test A,* n = 21 *for Tests B and C (95% confidence level).*

More than anything, these results indicate that question order impacts the nature of the responses given, which could lead to false conclusions in how the test data is interpreted.

Rule #7: Order the Questions Optimally

- The rules of good survey/questionnaire design regarding question order are in effect for five-second tests. Most importantly, make sure that the question order does not risk introducing bias into the results (see **Priming and Habituation**).
- To best leverage the participants' short-term memory, ask questions that require recall of specifics first (see **Memory fade and test format**).
- For target recall tests, order is extremely important. For attribute recall, it's less important. For opinion or emotional response, it's less important still (see **Does question order impact the ability to recall specific targets?**).

2.8 WRITING THE QUESTIONS

Murphy's Law states that "anything that can go wrong will go wrong." A common extension of this principle into the fields of writing, communication, and instructional design holds that "anything that can be misunderstood will be misunderstood." The way a question is worded will impact the meaning and intent of the question to the respondent and determine whether all respondents interpret the question the same way. Even subtle changes in question wording can affect the answers that people provide.

As with question order, there is a multitude of research and literature on the specifics of writing questions correctly, and it is beyond the scope of this book to delve into that research in any detail. However, before elaborating on some of the wording conditions commonly seen in five-second tests, a few key general points should be reiterated:

- Respondents who don't understand the questions will likely become alienated from the test and make little to no effort to respond accurately (see Section 2.3).
- The guiding principles for writing questions should always be relevance, clarity, precision, and a laser-like focus on what is intended to be learned (see Section 2.4).

- Use clear, simple language that respects the limitations of the method and its execution, is easily and correctly understood by the reader, and serves as a valid measure of what the researcher wants to learn (Redish, 2012).
- Design the questions to be good measures. Good questions maximize the relationship between the answers recorded and what the researcher is trying to measure (Fowler, 2002).
- Continuously pilot test the questions. Every question should be fine-tuned to reduce the likelihood of misunderstandings and misleading data (see Section 2.4).

Primed to Repeat

A surprisingly frequent mistake made in writing questions for five-second tests is priming the participant to simply repeat information given in the instructions. Section 2.4 discussed the importance of "proper" instructions, and that what makes instructions "proper" in a five-second test depends largely on (a) the test format and (b) the nature of questions that the participant will be asked to answer. Similarly, the researcher must ensure that the wording of the questions—especially the first one—considers the information that the participant has already been given in the instructions. Asking a question that encourages a simple repetition of previously stated information risks being a wasted effort, as in the following examples from actual tests:

Example 1
- **Instructions:** "Imagine that you are engaged and are browsing web sites about weddings."
- **Q1:** "What in particular is this site about?"

Example 2
- **Instructions:** "Imagine that you are interested in booking a luxury vacation."
- **Q1:** "What do you think the purpose of this site is?"

Example 3
- **Instructions:** "You are evaluating companies to hire for professional services."
- **Q1:** "What does this company do?"

These questions are not bad questions in and of themselves. Their presence suggests that each researcher seeks to confirm whether the product or service being offered is apparent and understood—a key objective of the five-second test. However, when the instructions contain a context statement (as on these examples), questions like these act as perfect setups for a simple restatement of that context:

- "The site is about weddings."
- "The purpose is to help someone book a luxury vacation."
- "The company provides professional services."

By not considering the wording of the question relative to the instructions, the researcher has squandered the point at which the participant's short-term memory is sharpest, the recall of details is most vivid, and the likelihood of getting useful data is highest.

There are two remedies for this condition, both of which require close attention to how the instructions and the questions work together. First, leave the wording of the questions alone but rewrite the instructions so that they are context-free. Using the first example, if the wording of the instructions is changed to some variation of "Remember as much as you can about the webpage you are about to see," responses to the question "What in particular is this site about?" will tell you whether or not the product or service is apparent. Unfortunately, despite the inclusion of the phrase *in particular*, the risk of a very general answer (e.g., "The site is about weddings") remains relatively high.

To get a better result, leave the wording of the instructions alone, but the rewrite the questions—including a reiteration of the context—so that they encourage the desired specificity:

Example 1
- **Instructions:** "Imagine you are engaged and browsing web sites about weddings."
- **Q1 (revised):** "What specific aspect of weddings does this site focus on?"

Example 2
- **Instructions:** "Imagine that you are interested in booking a luxury vacation."
- **Q1 (revised):** "What part of the vacation booking process is highlighted on this page?"

Example 3

- **Instructions:** "You are evaluating companies to hire for professional services."
- **Q1 (revised):** "What kind(s) of professional services does the company provide?"

By repeating the context within the question, you've beaten participants to the punch, so to speak—they should understand implicitly that a more specific answer is desired, and that recall of a specific detail will be required in order to deliver it.

Begging the Yes/No Answer

Previous sections of this book have noted the dangers of the yes/no question in five-second tests. This is an example of a dichotomous question, in which there can be only one of two answers (true/false is another example). As we've seen, they can be very tempting to use in five-second tests. They are popular with researchers because they are simple in concept, easy to ask, and lend themselves to easy coding and analysis of responses. Participants appreciate them because they are easy to understand and respond to with no more than three letters involved in submitting an answer, more short-term memory resources remain available for recall over a series of questions.

However, in five-second tests, they must be used with caution. Yes/no questions often force participants to choose between options that may not be that simple and may lead to participants deciding on an option that doesn't truly reflect their feelings. This is typically not a problem in attitudinal tests, where such answers act merely as validations of a respondent's opinion—either "yes, this statement does align with my opinion of the design" or "no, it does not." Conversely, for factual questions about what the participant saw in a test, yes/no data can be notoriously unreliable. Consider these examples from actual tests:

- "Did you notice the two buttons at the bottom of the page?"
- "Did you see where to buy the product?"
- "Did you find the information about downloading the mobile app?"

A diligent researcher would not be satisfied with the yes/no answers that these questions encourage. A more effective approach would be to reword the questions so that the participant must provide information that validates whether the answer is yes or no. This can be done by simply taking the journalistic approach of asking who, what, when, where, why, and how:

- "Where were the two buttons located?"
- "How can the product be purchased?"
- "What information do you remember about downloading the mobile app?"

Specific vs. General

A rule of thumb given by several of the online tool providers is: the more specific the questions are, the better. When considering how test questions are worded, a clear distinction should be made between a question that is *specific* and a question that is *unambiguous*. All questions should strive to have clear and accurate wording (i.e., be unambiguous), but specificity should be determined by knowing exactly what the researcher needs to learn (Rule #1) and what wording approach will best attain the desired result. In some cases, it's more useful to word questions more generally.

Consider this example, offered by one tool provider as a "simple, clear, specific" test question: "Did you see the free shipping offer?" (This question, of course, begs the yes/no answer, but we'll leave that aside for the time being.) The wording itself is indeed simple, clear, and unambiguous. The intent of the research, however, is less clear. One possibility is that the researcher wants to know merely if the design of the offer stands out visually (i.e., is noticeable) on the page; another is that (s)he wants to know whether a specific aspect of the offer (e.g., that shipping is free) is obvious. In each case, using the specific wording approach recommended by the tool will yield yes/no data that, as we've already seen, should be viewed with skepticism. On the other hand, wording the question more generally could provide data that tells the "true" story:

- In the case of design visibility, an alternate strategy is to ask the more general, "Name something that stands out visually on the page." The number of responses that mention the shipping offer will indicate whether the offer stands out visually.
- In the case of detail memorability, a general wording approach might ask, "What do you remember about the page specific to shipping?" Responses will help indicate whether the "free" aspect is remembered.

Vanity Checks

Designers make conscious decisions about what they include in a design—they want to set moods and expectations, emphasize particular elements, etc. Whether or not a design meets those goals is an opinion based on perception. Borrowing from the old saying, qualities like these are very much in the eye of the beholder. By including "vanity check" questions in a test, the researcher is seeking validation that the design will be perceived favorably by those who view it.

A good number of five-second test questions are devoted to validating the perceptual decisions made by designers, but of course "can you validate this decision?" cannot be asked in an actual test. There are other ways to measure first impression, reaction to look and feel, perceived clarity, etc. The good news is that there's generally a low risk of nonresponse answers to vanity check questions—giving an opinion on how a design is perceived is usually nonthreatening for the participant and easy to deliver. The challenge is to optimize wording strategies that result in more precise and usable data. Consider the following validation questions common in five-second tests and the strategy suggestions for getting the best results for each:

"What is your initial reaction to this page?" or **"What was your first impression of the design?"** This is a very natural "kick-off" question for a five-second test, regardless of format. Designers want to know what kinds of reactions their designs elicit, and what kinds of judgments are being made as a result (Chapter 3 will go into much greater detail about testing for emotional response). It is definitely a question worth asking for finished or near-finished designs, and asking it in these ways will usually result in useful responses. However, because the question is worded broadly, the responses may be inconsistent in nature and more time-consuming to categorize efficiently. To illustrate, the first impression feedback for the home page of an educational financing web site (Figure 2.13) was an almost equal mix of:

- Single-term descriptors ("energetic," "cluttered")
- Judgment statements ("It's bad," "no clear message")
- Factual comments ("has a lot of font-based elements," "multiple colored words")
- Explanatory remarks ("It takes time to find where to focus," "I had trouble understanding where I should look first")

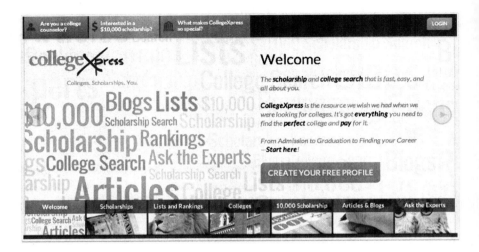

Figure 2.13 Education financing web site.

To get consistency in "first impression" data, word the question to prompt the desired data format. If you want to end up with a list of descriptors, ask the question: "What adjective immediately came to mind when the design appeared?" If you want a set of explanatory remarks for feedback, this way: "Explain your first thought when you first saw the page."

"Does the site look/seem professional?" There are two problems with using this question as written: first, of course, is the begging of the yes/no answer, which will result in relatively weak, meaningless data (unless there's a landslide either way). The second problem lies in the use of the word "professional," when more than likely what the researcher really wants to know is whether the design is perceived as being of high quality (attractive, engaging, and/or appropriate for the product, service, or company it represents).

This question would benefit from a rewrite that includes two corrective actions: the use of adjectives more specific to the quality that needs to be measured and employing a scale and numerical values for the response data: "Rate the attractiveness of the design on a scale from 1 to 10, where 10 = extremely attractive and 1 = extremely unattractive." In fact, you could use this approach to devote an entire test to design "quality," with each question focused on a specific aspect (however, you would need to guard closely against habituation).

"Is the product/service offering clear?" or **"Is it clear what this business is about?"** This question is a commonly used variation on the "professional look" question. Here again, confirming the characteristic is reduced to a simple yes/no choice, which provides no real insight as to whether the product or service is in fact readily apparent. Alternatively, using the wording "What is the product or service offered?" provides a way of measuring site intent with more precision and accuracy. A high percentage of correct responses will indicate that the product or service is clear; a high percentage of incorrect responses will indicate that it is not.

"Describe the design in a couple of words" or **"Give me a few words that describe the page."** Despite their initially benign appearance, these questions represent possible examples of question ambiguity. When asking questions like this, researchers are typically trying to compile a list of adjectives or descriptors that confirm a positive overall perception ("professional," "contemporary," "modern") or indicate a problematic one ("dull," "robotic," "boring"). Used "as is," these questions will produce a good number of descriptors; however, many respondents will instead supply short phrases that deviate from the desired data format and are not particularly useful (e.g., "it's OK," "looks fine," "nothing special," "it stinks"). Rewriting the question to read "Which two adjectives best describe the web site?" does more to ground the participant in exactly the type of response that the researcher wants. (Chapter 3 will outline an experiment in which changing the wording in this way more than doubled the number of test responses that provided two descriptors.)

Two Questions in One

This is a common condition in five-second tests. Standard survey design research preaches the importance of not asking compound questions (Kuniavsky, 2010), or questions that more than ask one question at a time. Sometimes this takes the form of "double-barrel" questions, which combine separate concepts in a single inquiry (e.g., "How much confidence do you have in your senator's ability to influence domestic *and* foreign policy affairs?"). Other times, it takes the form of consecutive questions, the second usually serving as a means of elaborating on the first:

- "What did you like? What changes would you make?"
- "Would you trust this site with your credit card? Why or why not?"
- "Would you change the navigation? If yes, how?"

The same "one question at a time" rule applies in five-second tests, regardless of whether they are administered in person or using an online tool. Combining questions in this way can lead to responses that are difficult to interpret. They are especially important in the online scenario, in which the text-entry response mechanisms encourage brevity in the writing of answers, then enforce it by setting character limits.

Rule #8: Pay Careful Attention to How the Questions are Worded

- In keeping with effective writing strategies, use simple, clear language that respects the reader. Pilot test questions to make sure there is a common understanding as to their meaning.
- Don't set the participant up to simply repeat the instructions. When instructions include a context statement, use references to that context to get more focused answers (see **Primed to repeat**).
- Yes/no questions may be useful for measuring attitudes or opinions, but not for factual information about what a participant saw or experienced (see **Begging the yes/no answer**).
- Specific questions are not always better than abstract questions. Know the difference between a *specific* question and an *unambiguous* question. Be aware of what you seek to learn from the data (see **Specific vs. general**).
- For "vanity check" questions, optimize wording strategies that result in more precise and usable data (see **Vanity checks**).
- Don't ask more than one question at a time (see **Two questions in one**).

2.9 ASKING ABOUT PROMINENCE

At first glance, asking a test participant to identify the most prominent element in a design seems reasonable. The question lends itself perfectly to the "view and react" mechanics of a five-second test—indeed, the skeptic might argue that identifying the most prominent element on a page is one of the few findings that the five-second test can deliver with any reliability. (That's probably why "understanding what customers remember most about your site" is touted as a key advantage of the method, and why the question is frequently included in online tools as a default or suggested question.)

The key to this question's viability, however, lies in whether or not asking it makes sense within the context of the design being tested. In a proper design context, asking the "most prominent" question can help confirm whether a page's purpose is obvious or can help designers understand trends in viewer perception in the presence of competing elements. In an improper design context, asking it risks doing little more than taking up space that could be used to ask something that would deliver more useful data.

Before proceeding further on this topic, an important distinction must be made. While they may imply the same general concept, asking "What is the most prominent element on the page?" is not the same as asking "What did you notice first on the page?" What one considers to be the most prominent item on a page can be changed based on reflection and further consideration of the design as a whole. What one notices first is not subject to further consideration—if answered truthfully, what is noticed first may not be what is determined to be the most prominent. When asking a participant the "most prominent" question, understand that the answer may not necessarily be what was noticed first.

The Case of Visual Dominance

Unless a design is in its very early stages of elaboration, it's likely that a good deal of thought has been given to which element is intended to be the most prominent. Hopefully, the decision has been made with the page or site's business goals in mind, e.g., if a design's primary goal is to enhance brand recognition, it should ensure that the brand logo or product name is the most prominent visual element. In such cases, asking the "most prominent" question most likely serves to confirm an explicit design decision, rather than to uncover something that is not already known or suspected. So, when visual dominance of a specific element is taken to the extreme, it becomes, in effect, a throwaway question.

Consider the example shown in Figure 2.14. The hi-res photo of the sunset has everything going for it in terms of visual prominence:

- it takes up a very large portion of the available space;
- it is positioned advantageously near the top;
- it stands in stark contrast to the subdued "light" font and the effective use of gray and white space on the rest of the page;
- as if size and position weren't enough to ensure prominence, the visual radiance of the setting sun acts as a visual beacon for the viewer, all but commanding the viewer to look at it.

Figure 2.14 Visual dominance in a design.

To assess the photo's prominence in this page design, it was tested in two separate five-second tests:

- When the "most prominent" question was asked as the first and only question in the test, 29 of 37 responses cited the photo.
- When it was asked as the third question in a sequence (testing the effects of memory fade), 31 of 37 responses cited the photo.

The results (Figure 2.15) indicate that, even with the impact on short-term memory caused by the presence of additional questions, the photo's visual dominance all but ensures that it is the most prominent element on the page.

So what useful data has the designer gained by asking the question within this particular context? One could argue (rather convincingly), not very much. With visual dominance making the answer this predictable, the design goals become irrelevant. A quick distribution of the design around the office, or to friends and family, would likely have provided the same results, so asking the question in a formal test with actual or representative customers amounts to a waste of time and effort.

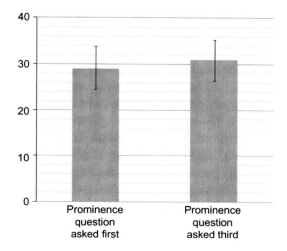

Figure 2.15 Prominence test in visual dominance, n = 37 (95% confidence).

Figure 2.16 Visual distribution in a design.

The Case of Visual Distribution

On the other hand, there's the case of a design in which the elements cause visual attention to be more distributed (Figure 2.16):

Here, a number of potential candidates are competing for prominence within the space:

- Two hi-res photos of an attractive and smiling person have specific advantages working in their favor. The smaller photo has the advantage of position in the upper left corner (numerous eyetracking studies confirm the "F-pattern" effect, in which viewers typically scan from left to right, starting in the upper left corner). The larger photo benefits from size, the visual inference of motion toward the center of the page, and the presence of secondary elements (e.g., the curling lines and green circles icons "emanating" from them).

- The product name "BabbaBox" also benefits from positioning on the left side of the page, as well as from the visual contrast against the light background and from the use of a very large font size.
- Perhaps less visually jarring (but still noteworthy), the orange box at the top provides a noticeable color contrast against the greens and browns used elsewhere on the page. It also contains "call to action" language that hints at a potential benefit for the viewer ("Win a free annual membership").

The effects of this visual competition are apparent when this design is tested using the same approach used in the example of visual dominance (Figure 2.17):

- In the single question test, 27 of 38 responses cited the "boxes" or "girl with the boxes" as the most prominent element. (The "BabbaBox" text was the most frequently cited of the other candidates, but all received at least 3–4 responses.)

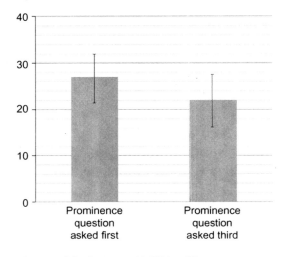

Figure 2.17 Prominence test in visual distribution, n = 38 (95% confidence).

• In the three-question test, 22 of 38 responses cited the larger photo—again, with a varied distribution among the other elements.

If the purpose of the page is to reinforce the brand or product recognition via the woman and her green boxes, the results provide confirmation that the design choices were good ones. If the purpose is to get people to sign up with the site via the free membership contest, the results suggest that the design should be reconsidered. The overall point is that when prominence is less easily predicted, asking the question has more validity and makes the test responses more meaningful.

Why the Five-Second Test Is Appropriate for Measuring Prominence

Chapter 1 explained how the five-second test is an ideal method for measuring visual perception in design. As the two examples used in this section have shown, visual prominence is the result of a number of perceptual factors—space, proximity, color, size, contrast, similarity, etc.—working together to establish the clear recognition of design elements and to facilitate focus, attention, and distinction. Five seconds is adequate for focusing on perception and limiting the introduction of other cognitive processes, which could alter what is perceived as prominent.

To measure how prominence might be impacted by these other processes, each of the previous designs were tested in an unmoderated "click test," in which participants were asked simply to view the image and click on what they considered to be the most prominent element, with no time restrictions. In both cases, the results were not nearly as predictable as they were in the five-second tests (Figures 2.18 and 2.19).

A closer look at the test data reveals that in each case, participants took considerably longer than 5 s to click on an element—an average of 9 s for the "boxes" design, and 16 s for the "sunset" design. Of course, given the unmoderated nature of the tests, there was no opportunity to determine whether any uncontrolled factors (e.g., computer performance or connectivity issues) accounted for the longer times. However, it's reasonable to assume that, with no time restriction and a reduced reliance on sensory input, participants felt free to spend time visually "exploring" the entire design and giving deliberate thought to the different elements before responding. Results using this method, therefore,

Figure 2.18 Heat map of click test results for prominence in the visual dominance design, n = 48.

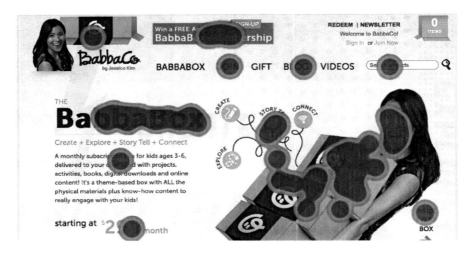

Figure 2.19 Heat map of click test results for prominence in the visual distribution design, n = 61.

would appear to be driven more by consideration than by sensory reaction, which runs counter to the true nature of prominence. (In fairness, the longer visual consideration occurring in a click test is more representative of what would occur in real life, so click test data might be a useful supplement to results received from a five-second test.)

Rule #9: Ask the "Most Prominent Element" Question with Discretion

- Use common sense. If it's obvious what the most prominent element in the design is, don't bother asking the question (unless you're simply looking for confirmation).
- If the question is asked, using the simpler wording, "What specific visual element stood out the most?" can help the participant focus on what makes the biggest visual impression, rather than what is visually dominant (although they may well be the same thing).
- If included in a multiquestion test, ask it as the last question in a three to four question sequence. Doing so will challenge the participant's available short-term memory, and the answer will more likely reflect what (s)he considers truly "prominent" (but be prepared for some "I don't remember" responses.)

2.10 OPEN-ENDED FEEDBACK

In most types of UX and design research, open-ended feedback is very often the goose that lays the golden egg. Getting participants to articulate their opinions in their own words allows them to reveal their likes and dislikes on their unique personal terms, within their own cognitive frameworks and often opens the door to new discoveries and considerations not considered previously. It's also a researcher's natural instinct to ask for it: having put a participant through a series of specific questions, asking for qualitative thoughts and opinions promises to add more color and "life" to the more structured responses.

However, harnessing the value of such feedback is difficult when there is no mechanism in place for maintaining control. In moderated sessions, the facilitator is there to guide the response and discussion, focus on the specific elements and contexts noted, and get a user back on track if the response wanders into unrelated areas. In unmoderated sessions, where the participant is free to provide only the level of detail that (s)he feels like providing, it's far more challenging to get a useful response.

The restrictive nature of unmoderated five-second testing tools compounds these difficulties—e.g., the uncustomizable response fields provided by the online testing tools. It is generally acknowledged that the size of a text-entry box will affect the amount of response that is given. The single line text-entry boxes provided by the online tool providers subliminally encourage brevity in the writing of answers, then enforce it by setting character limits. For the more focused questions we've seen so far, this is mostly not a problem, but given the more elaborative nature of the open-ended response, it makes the likelihood of getting useful data that much more challenging.

Still, researchers continue to ask for it. The corpus analyzed for this book show that roughly 9% of all tests ask for open-ended feedback in some way—usually as the last question in a four to five question sequence. As we'll see further in this section, the return on the effort usually isn't very high.

Roads to (Practically) Nowhere

Researchers generally use two approaches to asking for open-ended feedback in five-second tests—each of which, unfortunately, discourages elaborative thinking and provides an easy "path of least resistance" for moving closer to the end of a test.

First, there's the **"anything you care to tell me?"** strategy, as in:

- "Any additional feedback?"
- "Do you have any further comments that you would like to share?"

This type of question has the good intention of giving the participant free rein to provide *any* information—good, bad, or indifferent—that (s)he thinks the researcher should know and promises to reveal insights that the researcher does not anticipate. However, when the question is posed this way, most respondents tend to gravitate toward indifference. Experimentation with this approach shows that most respondents will "pass," "skip," answer in some form of "no," or simply provide a restatement of an earlier qualitative answer (e.g., "see my earlier comments").

The second strategy is the **request for change or improvement recommendations**, which can be posed in several ways. The most common approaches are:

- "Is there anything we could improve or change?"
- "Would you change anything about the page/design?"

Each of these questions suffer from one of the deficiencies discussed in Section 2.8, i.e., wording questions that beg the "yes" or "no" answer. It's worth stating again: when a question is worded in this way, it discourages the participant from giving the matter any further thought. As a researcher, the questions you ask should be focused on challenging the participant to provide something potentially useful, even if it ends up being a restatement of a previous comment. Anything that resonates with the participant enough that (s)he will bring it up again is likely to have some value, but you have to ask for it correctly to increase the chances of getting it.

There's also:

- "What change(s) would you make to the layout or design of this page?"
- "What if anything would you change to improve the design?"

This approach is only nominally better than the first. In each case, the easy pathway to the "no" answer has been merely replaced by an easy pathway to the "nothing" answer. The second example is especially egregious in this regard—inclusion of the phrase "if anything" gives the respondent an easy "out" for moving on to something else.

Finally, there's the more authoritative:

- "If you could change one thing about the page, what would it be?"
- "Suggest one positive change to improve the design."

Researchers who use this approach appear to understand the limitations facing them. The unmoderated nature of the tests means that there is no control in place for guiding the respondent toward a useful answer, and the single line text-entry response box provided by online test tools encourages brief responses. By asking the respondent to highlight a single aspect of the design, rather than the entirety of it, the researcher has given some incentive for providing a thoughtful response (albeit at the expense of more elaborative descriptions that open-ended feedback typically provide). In simpler terms, getting something is better than getting nothing.

Seldom Worth the Effort of Asking

Responses to open-ended feedback questions in a five-second test—regardless of the wording or the position of the question in the order—can be expected to be one of the following types.

Brief suggestions about a specific element existing on—or missing from—the page. For example:

- "Maybe move icons up just a little further above the fold."
- "Include a one sentence statement that instantly defines what the site does."
- "The illustration was freaky—tone it down."

These are the types of responses you're hoping for. Each focuses on a specific aspect of the design and speaks to what the respondent would consider to be an improvement. While each lacks the "why?" factor that is so important in open-ended feedback, they provide potentially important indications of areas that can be included in other forms of analysis and/or testing. Unfortunately, of the tests analyzed for this book, only about 20% of responses provide even this minimal level of detail. (Of course, there's nothing stopping you from asking "why is that?" if you have a subsequent question available in your test.)

General positive or negative comments about the overall design. Such responses can include:

- "Make it a little brighter"
- "Too much white for my liking"
- "It seemed pretty good to me"

These types of responses are far more representative of what you can expect in a five-second test. Their usefulness of course depends on what the researcher hopes to uncover: e.g., if there is suspicion that a design is too "plain," then several responses along the lines of "too much white" might be considered a research win. Generally speaking, however, they tend to be weak summative statements that either repeat a previously stated opinion or are indicative of a desire on the part of the participant to "just move along."

"Pass," or an explicit statement that "5 s is not enough time to answer this question." Here we get to the crux of the problem when asking for open-ended feedback in a five-second test. Regardless of how the question is worded, or how well positioned it is within the test structure, nothing can change the fact that the participant is given only five seconds' worth of exposure to the design (unless the testing mechanism allows for the customization of longer exposure times—but then it's no longer a five-second test, is it?).

If the design being tested is basic enough—say a single icon or logo, or a simple screen on a smart phone display—5 s may be enough time for a participant to retain enough detail to form an opinion and consider a possible alternative. Anything larger or more visually complex than that, and you're asking for something beyond the scope of what can be reasonably expected. It's simply not a fair question to ask of participants, and a good number of them will let you know it by providing nonresponses like this.

Your Best Bet

When considering the inclusion of an open-ended feedback question, remember Rule #1: don't use a five-second test if a different method is more appropriate. Getting good qualitative data requires having the proper mechanisms in place for participants to provide it—at the most basic level, that means giving them enough time to thoughtfully consider all elements of the design, then facilitating as elaborative a response as possible. Unmoderated five-second tests fail on both of these points.

However, if you are intent on asking the question, the best chances for getting useful feedback lie in the lessons of Rules #2 and 4. First, decide up-front that open-ended feedback is to be focus of the test and write the instructions accordingly: "As you view the following image, think about what you would change to make it better." Then simply ask the question: "What would you change about this design to make it better?" and expect a reference to one element or design aspect in the response. (If desired, you can use the remaining questions to ask for general comments/opinions on design look and feel, or to gather limited demographic data.) When approached in this manner, the likelihood of getting useful responses improves substantially.

Rule #10: Open-Ended Feedback Requests Carry a High Risk of Nonresponses and Low-Information Answers

- The nature of unmoderated sessions (lack of session control, restrictive tools, etc.) makes it more challenging to get useful responses from open-ended questions than from direct inquiry questions.
- Generally, 5 s is not a reasonable amount of time to expect the retention of details and consideration of alternative design approaches. Other methods are more effective for getting this type of data (see **Seldom worth the effort of asking**).
- If getting open-ended feedback using this method is important, ask for it in a highly focused test, restricted to asking for improvement recommendations (see **Your best bet**).

REFERENCES

Boyle, K.J., Welsh, M.P., Bishop, R.C., 1993. The role of question order and respondent experience in contingent-valuation studies. J. Environ. Econ. Manage. 25 (1), 80–99.

Brace, I., 2013. Questionnaire Design. Kogan Page, London.

Bradburn, N.M., Mason, W.M., 1964. The effect of question order on responses. J. Mark. Res. (JMR) 1 (4).

Chudoba, B., 2011. How much time are respondents willing to spend on your survey? SurveyMonkey Blog [blog]. 14 February, Available from: <https://www.surveymonkey.com/blog/en/blog/2011/02/14/survey_completion_times/> (accessed 21.11.13.).

Fowler, F.J., 2002. Survey Research Methods. Sage Publications, Thousand Oaks, CA.

How Habituation Can Negatively Affect Your Survey Reponses, 2011. SurveyMethods.com Survey Software Blog [blog]. 22 August 2011, Available from: <http://blog.surveymethods.com/how-habituation-can-negatively-affect-your-survey-reponses/> (accessed 08.09.13.).

Johnson, H., 2012. 10 tips to improve your online surveys. SurveyMonkey Blog [blog]. 13 April, Available from: <https://www.surveymonkey.com/blog/en/blog/2012/04/13/10-online-survey-tips/> (accessed 27.05.13.).

Kuniavsky, M., 2010. Observing the User Experience. Morgan Kaufmann, San Francisco, CA.

McFarland, S., 1981. Effects of question order on survey responses. Public Opin. Q. 45 (2), 208–215.

McKee, S., 2013. How to increase response rates for customer satisfaction surveys. SurveyGizmo Blog [blog]. 25 July, Available from: <http://www.surveygizmo.com/survey-blog/how-to-increase-response-rates-for-customer-satisfaction-surveys/> (accessed 22.09.13.).

Miller, G.A., 1956. The magical number seven, plus or minus two: some limits on our capacity for processing information. Psychol. Rev. 63 (2), 81.

Perfetti, C., 2013. Interview on Five-Second Testing. Interviewed by Paul Doncaster [by phone]. 1 February 2013.

Redish, J., 2012. Letting Go of the Words, second ed. Morgan Kaufmann, Waltham, MA.

RECOMMENDED READING

Albert, B., Tullis, T., Tedesco, D., 2010. Beyond the Usability Lab. Morgan Kaufmann, San Francisco, CA.

Courage, C., Baxter, K., 2005. Understanding Your Users. Morgan Kaufmann Publishers, Amsterdam.

Fowler, F.J., 1995. Improving Survey Questions. Sage Publications, Thousand Oaks, CA.

Kuniavsky, M., 2010. Observing the User Experience. Morgan Kaufmann, San Francisco, CA.

Schade, A., 2013. Remote Usability Tests: Moderated and Unmoderated Nngroup.com [online]. Available from: <http://www.nngroup.com/articles/remote-usability-tests/> (accessed 30.10.13.).

Schwarz, N., 1999. Self-reports: how the questions shape the answers. Am. Psychol. 54 (2), 93.

CHAPTER 3

Testing for Emotional Response

Oscar Wilde. Will Rogers. A popular brand of dandruff shampoo.

Each has been referenced as the origin of one of our most closely held modern anxieties: "You never get a second chance to make a first impression." While the true source of its origin may not ultimately matter, the concept itself has taken a firm hold in the world of product design—and, consequently, in the central concerns of marketing, sales, executive leadership, and any other stakeholder interested in a product's bottom line. An increased emphasis on creating a favorable first impression means an increased pressure on UX and visual designers to define and measure **emotional response**.

In his book *Designing for Emotion*, Aaron Walter (2011) describes **emotional design** as a logical extension of Maslow's famous hierarchy of human needs, which hypothesizes that satisfying human needs is a sequential process, starting with the lower levels (physiological and safety requirements) and moving on to higher-level needs, such as appreciation of aesthetics. Extended to the use of products (online or otherwise), the central idea is that a product must establish a sense of functionality, reliability, and usability (e.g., addressing the lower-level needs) before a user can recognize its perceptual aspects as contributing to its overall **desirability**.

However, an increasing number of studies suggest that establishing desirability is largely a matter of first impression and will not necessarily wait for the satisfaction of the lower-level needs. The title of a frequently cited Canadian study (Lindgaard et al., 2006) sets an extremely narrow margin for error: "You have 50 milliseconds to make a first impression." A 2011 eye-tracking study (Sheng et al., 2011) suggests a slightly more generous—but no less onerous—180 ms. Such evidence points to first impressions—favorable or otherwise—being formed instantaneously, almost entirely via the perceptual senses, and suggests that the risks of ignoring the criticality of first impressions are huge.

Numbers of milliseconds aside, there are two reasons why researchers should care deeply about creating favorable first impressions through design. First, they impact a product or application's *perceived* (actual) ability to meet the lower-level needs of the user and thus help create immediate connections with users on a personal level. Second, an inability to elicit critical positive emotions (joy, serenity, interest, hope, amusement, inspiration), which forge positive behaviors, means a greater likelihood of eliciting negative emotions (dislike, agitation, indifference, boredom, discouragement, animosity) that forge negative behaviors. If users have a positive first impression of the design aesthetics, they are more likely to overlook or forgive poor usability or limited functionality (Kurosu and Kashimura, 1995), and can go so far as motivating increased registrations, completed transactions, etc. With a negative impression, users are more likely to find fault with the interactions of a site or product, even if its overall usability is good and the product offers real value.

There is arguably a fine line between emotional response and first impression, depending on how one chooses to define them. They can be seen as interchangeable concepts, each referring to what one feels upon immediate exposure to a product. Alternatively, they can be differentiated by requiring distinct degrees of meaningful interaction with a product. Whatever the definitions, visual perceptions of a design, and the initial reactions they elicit, undoubtedly influence the connection a user will make with a product—which means that five-second tests (when used appropriately) can play a role in determining whether that connection is positive or negative.

3.1 COMMON APPROACHES IN FIVE-SECOND TESTS

Most of the tests analyzed for this book included some degree of emotional response inquiry, usually in the form of one or more questions included within a mixed test format. Typically, these questions made use of the word "feel" in an attempt to tap into a participant's sense of awareness regarding a design:

- "In one word, how does the design make you feel?"
- "What is the general feeling you get out of the page?"
- "What is your overall feeling when you first see the site?"
- "What does the site's design make you feel about the company?"

Another common strategy seen in the sample asked respondents to describe first reactions in their own words:

- "What are one or two words you would use to describe the look and feel of the site?"
- "How would you describe the personality of this site?"
- "What was your first impression(s) of this application?"
- "What is the first thing that comes to mind when you viewed this page?"

Less frequently, questions were worded as direct solicitations of whether a design triggers an innately positive or negative reaction:

- "Does the site design appeal to you?"
- "Is there anything particularly gratifying about the design?"
- "What was most off-putting about the design of this web site?"
- "Did something about the design bother you?"

The problem with trying to gauge emotional response this way correlates directly with the problems with the mixed, or unfocused, format—i.e., when trying to measure several things in a single test, there is a greater risk for getting suboptimal data, and greater attention must be paid to how a test is constructed. A more effective approach would be to adhere strictly to an attitudinal test format, as outlined in Section 2.2. Very few tests analyzed for this book took this approach, but here's an example of one that did:

Instructions: "Please view the site to rate its visual style and appearance (Figure 3.1)."

Q1. "Give a rating from 0 to 5: 0 = 'ugly,' 5 = 'beautiful')"
Q2. "Give a rating from 0 to 5: 0 = 'shady,' 5 = 'trustworthy')"
Q3. "Give a rating from 0 to 5: 0 = 'dated,' 5 = 'modern')"
Q4. "Rate your comfort with sending money on this site 0−5: 0 = 'no way,' 5 = 'comfortable')"
Q5. "Imagine you were a customer of this site and it worked perfectly. Assuming your friends needed this service, based on style alone, how likely are you to recommend the service 0−5: 0 = 'no chance,' 5 = 'very likely')?"

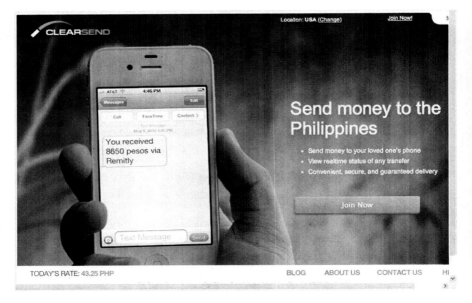

Figure 3.1 Design image for test consisting solely of emotional response questions.

On the whole, this represents a fairly well constructed test:

- It correctly aligns with, and adheres to, the attitudinal format.
- The instructions are effective, in that they directly address what the participant is expected to do—render an opinion on items of perception.
- The test image has not been optimized to eliminate scrolling completely; however, a quick look at the scrollbars indicates that only a very small percentage of the total image is not visible, so there is enough to judge the design in its totality.
- Q1 and Q3 each ask for the participant's opinion concerning the page's aesthetic appeal. They are consistent with the expectation set in the instructions and make effective use of a rating scale featuring opposing design values.
- Q2 and Q4 are constructed similarly to the others, but rather than focusing on different aspects of aesthetic appeal, each speaks to the perception of trustworthiness (Q2 does so directly, while Q4 does so by inference). Trustworthiness is certainly related to emotional response but requires a more nuanced approach to test with any effectiveness. (Chapter 4 will deal with testing for trust and credibility in more detail.)

- Only Q5 is truly problematic, for multiple reasons (use of an unrealistic context, asking to predict future behavior, long and complex wording of the question), and should not be included.

3.2 ITERATING A VIABLE FIVE-SECOND TEST APPROACH

With such close ties to both visual perception and attitudinal inquiry based on short exposure times, emotional response appears to be ideally suited for adaptation to the five-second test method. The issue, of course, is how best to execute it. As mentioned previously, a mixed test format risks suboptimal results. A memory dump test might provide some sense of emotional response, but simply asking "what did you remember?" is more likely to result in target identification data.

The attitudinal format is the obvious choice for this type of questioning, but the standard line of questioning can be further enhanced by borrowing from an established method for testing for emotional response. In a series of presentations on measuring emotional response, Hawley (2010) describes a process of first determining brand attributes and their opposites, then using product reaction cards (Benedek and Miner, 2002) to see which positive and negative words test participants use to describe a site or design. Using a survey tool, participants were first shown a page design option, then were asked to describe the design by selecting five adjectives from a list of 60. (They were also given an opportunity to explain why they made the choices they did.) By tabulating the submitted positive and negative attributes per design, researchers can measure how closely a design stimulus achieves the desired reaction.

Obviously, the use of product reaction cards does not fit within the confines of an online five-second test. However, the idea of using descriptor words to confirm or contradict attributes that the stakeholders seek to have aligned with their design can be accommodated in a single test. After some iteration, a modification of Hawley's approach was developed to provide a template for obtaining an effective mix of qualitative and quantitative emotional response data:

- During test preparation, stakeholders identify two to four design values that they assume or desire the tested design to represent, as well as their opposites. For example, a law firm wanting to present an image of being a reliable and tenacious advocate might use the following value pairs:

- stable/unreliable
- competent/inept
- determined/hesitant

- In the first phase of a test, participants are asked to provide two descriptor words that they believe best describe the design. Doing so allows them to relate their own personal connection to the design in their own words. From an analysis standpoint, it allows the researcher to both (a) divide the descriptors into categories of positive/complimentary, negative/disparaging, or neutral and (b) get direct confirmation or contradiction of any of the established design values, or their opposites.
- In the second phase, participants are prompted to provide a rating for each preidentified design value on a scale, with the desired value on one end and its opposite on the other. This approach puts the participants' focus on each value for consideration individually and allows them to "plot" their choice easily using a number value.

3.3 TESTING THE TEMPLATE

A pilot test of this approach was set up using the home page of a financial services firm. In a purely fictional research scenario, the stakeholders hope that the following design values are confirmed:

- **Professional:** the design should represent a company that values and insists on competence and skill in everything they do.
- **Clear:** the design should present information free from clutter and with relative transparency.
- **Stimulating:** the design should motivate the viewer enough to initiate further investigation of the site and its information.
- **Reassuring:** the design should elicit a sense of approachability and confidence in the firm as a provider of quality services.

The pilot test was constructed as follows:

Instructions: "You are in the market for a personal financial planner when you come across this site. After viewing a page for 5 s, you'll be asked for your reaction to the design (Figure 3.2)."

Figure 3.2 Emotional response test image, for financial services web site.

Q1. "What two words would you use to describe the appearance of this site?"

Q2. "Provide a rating for this design, from 1 to 5: 1 = Professional, 5 = Amateurish"

Q3. "Provide a rating for this design, from 1 to 5: 1 = Confusing, 5 = Clear"

Q4. "Provide a rating for this design, from 1 to 5: 1 = Stimulating, 5 = Dull"

Q5. "Provide a rating for this design, from 1 to 5: 1 = Intimidating, 5 = Reassuring"

Note that the numerical assignments of the design values and their opposites alternate within the scales. In Q2 and Q4, the desired values are assigned "1," with the opposites assigned "5"; in Q3 and Q5, the assignments are reversed. This approach is not necessary but can help lessen the likelihood of habituation or repetition of answers (see Section 2.7).

Upon completion of the test, the nonprompted descriptors were visualized in a word cloud (Figure 3.3), using a free tool available at http://www.wordle.net/. In terms of alignment with the stated design values, the data show instances of both corroborative and contradictory descriptors:

- **Professional:** 7 of 21 respondents used the word "professional" to describe the design.

Figure 3.3 Word cloud representation of emotional response descriptors, n = 21.

- **Clear:** Responses were largely devoid of any measurement either way on the clarity value, with responses indicating that the design is "clean" and "cluttered" canceling each other out.
- **Stimulating:** There is some problem with the stated design value of "stimulating" via indications that the design is "bland" or "vanilla."
- **Reassuring:** This value was noted in only two responses using the words "trustworthy" and "legitimate"; no responses indicated any sentiment to the contrary.

Overall, 11 of 32 nonprompted descriptors were categorized as positive, with another 11 categorized as neutral, and the remainder as negative descriptors. With only a quarter of the unprompted responses being negative, this set of data may be interpreted as indicative of an overall positive-to-neutral emotional response to the design.

However, the intent of Q1 ("What two words would you use to describe the appearance of this site?") was to compile a list of adjectives or descriptors that confirm the positive design values (or indicate design problems by confirming the opposites). As discussed in Section 2.8 regarding the writing of test questions, the wording of Q1 ("What *two words* would you use to describe the appearance of this site?") is not specific enough to keep some respondents from deviating from the desired data format or providing answers that are not particularly useful:

- 9 of 21 responses consisted of two descriptors, as expected
- 5 of 21 responses consisted of a single descriptor
- 7 of 21 responses consisted of a phrase of two or more words ("stock photos," "old school," "too cluttered," "nothing comes to mind")

The results of the scale ratings are visualized in a series of graphs (Figure 3.4), in which the shaded areas indicate the user response rates.

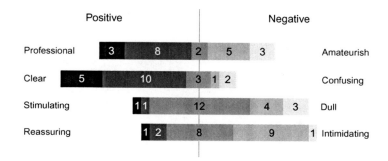

Figure 3.4 Scale results for design value ratings, n = 21.

These results indicate that respondents generally affirmed the design values of "professional" and "clear," while raising some question as to whether the design is "stimulating" or "reassuring."

To further test the template, this test was replicated using a content page from the web site of a family health club. In an effort to improve the data for the nonprompted responses, Q1 was rewritten to ask: "What two *adjectives* would you use to describe the appearance of this site?" The goal in making this change was to cut down on single descriptor responses and multiword phrases, and produce more responses containing two descriptors. The design values were also changed to align better with the atmosphere a family health club might wish to promote:

* professional
* easygoing
* modest
* reassuring

Instructions: "You are researching health clubs when you come across this site. Be prepared to state how the design makes you feel about the club (Figure 3.5)."

Q1. "What two adjectives would you use to describe the general appearance of this site?"
Q2. "Provide a rating for this design, from 1 to 5: 1 = Professional, 5 = Amateurish"
Q3. "Provide a rating for this design, from 1 to 5: 1 = Easygoing, 5 = Assertive"
Q4. "Provide a rating for this design, from 1 to 5: 1 = Pretentious, 5 = Modest"

Figure 3.5 Emotional response test image, for health club web site.

Q5. "Provide a rating for this design, from 1 to 5: 1 = Intimidating, 5 = Reassuring"

As predicted, the change of wording used in Q1 resulted in an improvement in the response data. While there was not nearly as much confirmation of the exact design values and opposites as in the first experiment, instances of responses containing two descriptor words jumped from 9 of 21 responses to 19 of 20 responses. (This result does not mean to imply that a change in wording strategy will guarantee better results but does support the idea that wording specificity can increase the chances of getting the data you want.) 18 of 38 descriptor words submitted in Q1 were negative, indicating an overall neutral-to-negative response to the design, given the desired design values. The rating scale results for Q2–Q5 (Figure 3.6) showed that respondents generally affirmed the design value of "professional" but also gave support to the opposing values of "assertive," "pretentious," and "intimidating."

With these sets of data in hand, the researcher is able to not only quantify the success of a design against company and/or stakeholder values but also get a richer idea of how the design is perceived (and

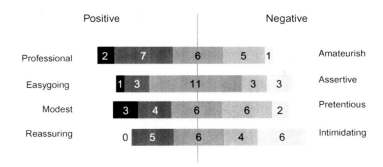

Figure 3.6 Scale results for design value ratings. n = 21.

point the way to possible improvements) by having respondents describe what they're seeing *in their own descriptive words*. At minimum, this template for using the five-second test for emotional response provides a much more robust means of evaluating first impressions than simply including one or more attitudinal questions in a mixed format test. However, to reiterate a point made at the outset of the book, using the five-second test method for emotional response testing should not be considered as the be-all and end-all. While it can help settle design disputes within a product team and get you pointed in the right direction, results should be used as the starting point for determining whether longer exposures to the design confirm positive first impressions hold and/or alleviate negative first impressions.

Recommended test template for emotional response testing

1. During test planning, identify up to four values that the company or designer wishes to convey in the page or site design.
2. Test instructions should follow the attitudinal approach for providing opinion-based responses. (Context statements are acceptable, as long as they are not unrealistic.)
3. In the first test question, ask the participant to provide *adjectives* (no more than three) that best describe the design.
4. All remaining questions ask the participant to assign a rating to a targeted value and its opposite: "Provide a rating for this design, from 1 to 5: 1 = corporate value, 5 = corporate value opposite." To guard against habituation, consider alternating the positions of the values and opposites on the rating scales. To compensate for potential ordering effects, consider randomizing the order in which the word pairs are presented.

5. Once the test has concluded, categorize the descriptors submitted for the first question as positive, negative, or neutral; make note of how many provide a direct or indirect match against the design values or opposites.
6. Create graphs that visualize the scale ratings given to the values and opposites in the remaining questions and compare the two data sets to determine the overall emotional response to the design.

REFERENCES

Benedek, J., Miner, T., 2002. Measuring Desirability: New Methods for Evaluating Desirability in a Usability Lab Setting, paper presented at UPA 2002 Conference, 8–12 July, Orlando, FL. Available from: <http://www.pagepipe.com/pdf/microsoft-desirability.pdf>.

Hawley, M., 2010. Rapid Desirability Testing: A Case Study: UXmatters' Uxmatters.com. [online]. Available from: <http://www.uxmatters.com/mt/archives/2010/02/rapid-desirability-testing-a-case-study.php>.

Kurosu, M. and Kashimura, K. 1995. "Apparent usability vs. inherent usability: experimental analysis on the determinants of the apparent usability", CHI '95 Conference Companion on Human Factors in Computing Systems, Denver, CO, 7-11 May. New York: ACM, pp. 292–293.

Lindgaard, G., Fernandes, G., Dudek, C., Brown, J., 2006. Attention web designers: you have 50 milliseconds to make a good first impression! Behav. Inf. Technol. 25 (2), 115–126.

Sheng, H., Lockwood, N. S., Dahal, S., 2011. Eyes Don't Lie: Understanding Users' First Impressions on Websites Using Eye Tracking, paper presented at HCI International'13, 21–26 July 2013, Las Vegas, NV, pp. 635–641.

Walter, A., 2011. Designing for Emotion. A Book Apart/Jeffrey Zeldman, New York, NY.

RECOMMENDED READING

Anderson, S.P., 2011. Seductive Interaction Design. New Riders, Berkeley, CA.

Boehm, N., 2010. Organized Approach to Emotional Response Testing|UX Magazine [online]. Available from: <https://uxmag.com/articles/organized-approach-to-emotional-response-testing> (accessed 20.12.13).

Inchauste, F., 2011. UX is 90% Desirability. GetFinch [blog]. 10 March 2011, Available from: <http://www.getfinch.com/2011/03/ux-is-mostly-desirability/> (accessed 22.12.13).

Norman, D.A., 2004. Emotional Design. Basic Books, New York, NY.

Van Gorp, T., Adams, E., 2012. Design for Emotion. Elsevier/Morgan Kaufmann, Boston, MA.

Van Schaik, P., Ling, J., 2009. The role of context in perceptions of the aesthetics of web pages over time. Int. J. Hum. Comput. Stud. 67 (1), 79–89.

CHAPTER 4

Testing for Trustworthiness and Credibility

Chapter 3 noted an interpretational fine line between emotional response and first impression. The same can be said of **trustworthiness** and **credibility**—terms that are often used interchangeably. Arguments abound as to which one takes precedence and/or leads to the other. One may say that trust is a component of the larger concept of credibility; e.g., if information can be proven in some quantitative way to have value as a result of its reliability or trustworthiness, it may be said to be credible. On the other hand, it may also be said that because credibility may be quantified, it is a contributing factor (along with reliability, sincerity, and competence) to the larger concept of trust. Ultimately, the link between trust and credibility is likely a subjective matter of definition. What cannot be denied is that both trust and credibility are made possible only as the result of a positive reaction to a product or service. As we saw with emotional response, first impression can play a big role in creating that reaction.

Noted persuasive design expert Fogg (2003) has described four levels of credibility that influence positive judgments about a web site or online product. Three of these levels require delving into deeper aspects of overall user experience, such as the information source's name recognition, reputation, perceived motive, affiliations, and advertising relationships. A good many of these aspects require some degree of prior experience interacting with a site at multiple levels (how current the content is, page load times, grammatical and/or spelling errors, transparency of information about the company and its key personnel, etc.). The link to visual perception (and thus to the use of the five-second test to gauge trustworthiness) lies in the level that Fogg calls **surface credibility**. That which can be perceived immediately (colors, layout, images, etc.) has the ability to boost credibility substantially—e.g., the use of "stock photos" or public domain imagery can have a negative effect on perceived credibility, while using "real" images can help communicate a sense of authenticity and legitimacy.

Designers are rightly concerned that their designs should project trustworthiness and credibility, and that concern is borne out by industry experts. In one of Fogg's more famous studies (Fogg et al., 2003), participants were allowed to spend as much time as they wanted looking at a collection of web sites, with ample opportunity to have their perceptions of trust influenced by core site content, marketing messages, contextual help, and other components of "direct" persuasion. Yet, in the end, his analysis showed that the highest percentage of participant comments—greater than 46%—referenced "design look" as a critical component in establishing credibility. Likewise, Nielsen (1999) has noted that the "indirect" component of overall "design quality"—which includes professional appearance, conveyance of respect for customers, and implications of good service—is one of the primary ways that a web site can communicate trustworthiness.

4.1 COMMON APPROACHES IN FIVE-SECOND TESTS

It should then come as no surprise that roughly a quarter of the five-second tests analyzed for this book included at least one question relating to trust (17%) or credibility (7%). Most inquiries were included as single, dichotomous questions in attitudinal or mixed format tests, referencing explicitly the concept of trust:

- "Do you **trust** this web site?"
- "Is this web site **trustworthy**?"
- "Would you **trust** this web site with your e-mail address/credit card information?"

A lesser percentage took an indirect approach, invoking one or more attributes that can contribute to a sense of trustworthiness or credibility:

- "Would you recognize this site as an **authority**?"
- "Based on first impressions, would you feel **confident** buying products from this company?"
- "Rate your **comfort** with sending money on this site 0–5: 0 = 'no way,' 5 = 'comfortable')."

Researchers not only are asking about trustworthiness as a design attribute but are doing so with a fair degree of priority. More than half of all inquiries related to trust were asked within the first three

Figure 4.1 Design image for test consisting solely of trust/credibility questions.

questions. Further, for many it is not enough to know whether or not a design conveys trustworthiness—a good number also want to know why (by tacking "why or why not?" at the end of the question).

Only one test in the sample appeared to be focused solely on trust.

Instructions: "We are going to show you the home page of a business financial health evaluation service. This service is aimed at large companies (Figure 4.1)."

Q1. "What are your first impressions, in a few words?"

Q2. "Does it look: professional, trustworthy (sic), encouraging to read more?"

Q3. "Would you trust the service with your financial data and predictions it creates for your business?"

Q4. "What would you like to see to commit further?"

Analysis shows a number of problems that add up to a generally poorly constructed test:

- The instructions give notice to what will be shown and provide some details about the service. However, they do not set the expectation for *delivering opinions* on visual aspects of the design. Absent this expectation, viewers are likely to attempt focusing on specific target elements at first, rather than on the overall impression made by the page's design. (However, in this specific case, the text-heavy page creates a case of competing visual elements, which makes a focus on specific targets difficult anyway.)
- The image is cropped but is still large enough to require scrolling in most monitor resolutions.
- Q1 takes the recommended approach outlined in the emotional response template, asking for participant reaction to the design in their own words before moving on to more targeted questions.
- Q2 is an example of a double-barrel question (see Section 2.1)—or, more accurately, a "triple-barrel" question, since the question asks for consideration of three design values instead of two. This is a violation of sound survey practice.
- Q3 is, quite simply, a wasted question. Rather than focusing on the emotions that the *design* elicits, the wording focuses on the perceived trustworthiness of the *company* as an entity. Trust in an entity (especially one associated with money management) requires some meaningful transactional experience over time and certainly cannot be measured based on 5 s worth of exposure to a design (similar to the issue of quality described in the quinceneara web site example of Section 2.3). This question is almost guaranteed to deliver a large number of "no," "I don't know," and "I cannot answer this" responses.
- Q4 is a variation on suggestions for improvement to a design (see Section 2.10) but is framed within the context of establishing a greater sense of comfort and trust, which (hopefully) would result in the intended positive outcome of "committing further." This of course represents an unreasonble request on the part of the researcher—generally, 5 s is not a reasonable amount of time to expect the retention of details and consideration of alternative design approaches.

4.2 ITERATING A VIABLE FIVE-SECOND TEST APPROACH

Most established questionnaires used in conjunction with formal usability testing are devoid of references to trustworthiness. For example, the System Usability Scale (Brooke, 1996) and the Website Analysis and MeasureMent Inventory (WAMMI—Home, n.d.) contain few, if any, questions that focus on the perception of credibility. However, the Standardized Universal Percentile Rank Questionnaire (SUPR-Q: Standardized Universal Percentile Rank, n.d), developed by Jeff Sauro, takes a more cohesive approach by including measures for usability, loyalty, appearance, *and* credibility. The questionnaire contains several statements that speak specifically to trustworthiness, value, and comfort as perceptual cues:

- "I feel comfortable purchasing from this web site." (references a sense of comfort, contentment, and being at ease)
- "This web site keeps the promises it makes to me." (references the appearance of dependability and reliability)
- "I can count on the information I get on this web site." (references the projection of honesty, sincerity, and transparency)
- "I feel confident conducting business with this web site." (references the sense of confidence, self-assurance, and empowerment a participant feels when interacting with a design)

At first glance, these statements appeared to be viable "as is" as a complete template for five-second testing. To test their viability, they were included in a series of four preliminary tests—two tests using the landing pages of online shopping sites, and two using the home pages of antiques/memorabilia dealers. The tests were constructed as follows:

- The order in which the statements were presented was changed in each test, to ensure that question order did not impact results.
- For the sake of simplicity, the response options for each statement were limited to "agree," "disagree," or "no opinion." (For the purposes of this experiment, "no opinion" was counted as a nonresponse.)
- In all tests, a fifth question was asked at the end of the statement sequence: "If you answered 'no opinion' to any of the previous questions, what is the reason for giving that answer?" The goal of this final question was to determine whether, from the participant standpoint, any of the statements is unreasonable to ask within the confines of a five-second test, and if so, why.

The cumulative results for all four tests ($n = 83$) indicate that, indeed, some aspects of credibility evoke responses with greater reliability than others when using the five-second test method:

- "I feel comfortable purchasing from this web site." (13 of 83 were nonresponses)
- "This web site keeps the promises it makes to me." (57)
- "I can count on the information I get on this web site." (31)
- "I feel confident conducting business with this web site." (17)

These results undoubtedly reflect the nature of the questions asked. By using the word "feel," Q1 and Q4 are structured to invoke the personal reactions that participants had to the design. Conversely, Q2 references a concept that requires some degree of transactional experience in order to answer, while Q3 requires some meaningful interaction with the information, which cannot be accommodated within 5 s (except when past experience and reputation are contributing factors).

Analysis of the responses to Q5 indicates that respondents did not consider the time restrictions of the five-second test to be a major contributor to their submission of "no opinion" responses. Of the total number of respondents ($n = 57$) who provided an answer to Q5, only 15 said that 5 s is not enough time to render an opinion on any of the presented statements. Higher numbers of respondents referenced nonperceptible aspects of trustworthiness (33)—e.g., lack of previous experience with site—or deficiencies in the design aesthetics of the specific sites tested (22) as the reason for their nonresponses. It would appear then that a five-second exposure to a design is not perceived as a barrier to asking at least some questions related to trustworthiness.

Taken together, these results help point the way toward a viable template for using the five-second test to gauge initial perceptions of trustworthiness and credibility. Recall from the emotional response template the requirement that stakeholders identify which design values they assume or desire the tested design to represent. The same approach can be used here:

- During test preparation, stakeholders identify value options that contribute specifically to trust and credibility (e.g., putting the viewer at ease, projecting honesty and/or sincerity, and empowering the user to proceed with confidence).

- Statements are crafted that put the focus on the ability of the design to elicit the stated values. It is important that each statement focus on a *single* value, rather than including closely related elements—e.g, dependability and reliability—in the same statement (see Section 2.8 on avoiding double-barrel questions). It is equally important that the statement focus explicitly on the *design* (i.e., what the viewer sees in the test) rather than the company, product, or service featured (which cannot be "experienced" in a five-second test).
- In the actual test, participants are prompted to respond to each value, either by selecting a response option or by providing a rating on a Likert scale (value opposites may be used on the scale, if desired). This puts the participants' focus on each value for consideration individually, allows them to "plot" their choice easily, and lessens the possibility of nonresponses.

4.3 TESTING THE TEMPLATE

A pilot test of this approach was set up using the home page of a small financial services firm (to lessen the likelihood of influence by name recognition, reputation, etc.). In this purely fictional research scenario, the stakeholders have decided that they wish the design to evoke a sense of dependability, honesty, and a dedication on customer needs. Once again, the "agree/disagree/no opinion" response options were used.

Instructions: "As you view the page snapshot, think about how the design look and feel represents the company (Figure 4.2)."

Q1. "The design reflects a company that is dependable. Agree, disagree, or no opinion?"

Q2. "The design reflects a company that is ethical. Agree, disagree, or no opinion?"

Q3. "The design reflects a company that is sensitive to the needs of its customers. Agree, disagree, or no opinion?"

The results of this test (Figure 4.3) showed initial positive indicators for the company being perceived as ethical (7 agree, 4 disagree) and concerned meeting the needs of customers (9 agree, 5 disagree), but not dependable (4 agree, 7 disagree). Since the aim was to get a general sense of perceived trustworthiness and credibility, stakeholders could use the data (along with the relative "no opinion" responses) as a

Figure 4.2 *Credibility test image, for small financial services firm web site.*

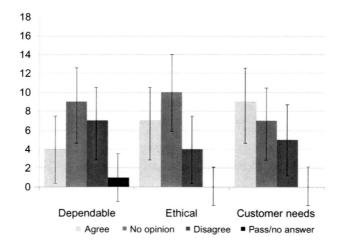

Figure 4.3 *Results of financial services company credibility test,* n = 21 *(95% confidence level).*

starting point for discussions on where (if any) design improvements need to addressed and tested in further research efforts.

Of course, results of the first test may well have been influenced by the choice of the business represented—as noted earlier, financial firms are particularly vulnerable to hesitation and/or discretion when it comes to perception of trustworthiness. To get a different take, the

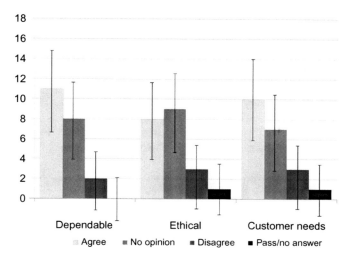

Figure 4.4 Results of moving company credibility test, n = 21 *(95% confidence level).*

pilot test was repeated using the "Services" page of a regional moving company. All test elements (instructions, value options, response options, etc.) were kept in place. The results of this test (Figure 4.4) showed initial positive indicators for all three value contributors to the company's perceived credibility.

As with testing for emotional response, researchers can use this template approach to quickly quantify the degree to which a design elicits feelings of trustworthiness and credibility. However, the same cautions apply as well—while using the five-second test can create a starting point for design discussions, it should not be used as decision-making exercise, or as substitute for more rigorous research that dives deeper into the intricacies of creating that critical impression of trustworthiness.

Recommended test template for trust/credibility testing

1. During test planning, identify and prioritize which element(s) of trustworthiness and credibility are to be measured.
2. Test instructions should follow the attitudinal approach of putting the participant in the proper frame of mind for delivering opinion-based responses. (Context statements are unnecessary and discouraged in this case.)

3. While it does not hurt the test to ask participants to describe the design in their own words, responses are not likely to relate to elements of trust or credibility and therefore should be discouraged.
4. Provide one test question per identified element, using a numerical rating scale or a defined set of options to register responses. Take care not to include closely related elements (e.g, dependability and reliability) in the same question.
5. Create graphs that visualize the scale ratings given to the elements to determine the overall sense of trustworthiness/credibility that the design elicits.

REFERENCES

Brooke, J., 1996. SUS: a "quick and dirty" usability scale. In: Jordan, P.W., Thomas, B., Weerdmeester, B.A., McClelland, A.L. (Eds.), Usability Evaluation in Industry. Taylor and Francis, London, pp. 189—194.

WAMMI—Home [online]. Available from: <http://www.wammi.com/> (accessed 21.03.13.).

Fogg, B.J., 2003. Persuasive Technology. Morgan Kaufmann Publishers, Amsterdam.

Fogg, B.J., Soohoo, C., Danielson, D., Marable, L., Stanford, J., Tauber, E., 2003. How do users evaluate the credibility of web sites? A study with over 2,500 participants, paper presented at DUX2003, Designing for User Experiences Conference, 5—7 June 2003, San Francisco, CA.

Nielsen, J., 1999. Trust or Bust: Communicating Trustworthiness in Web Design Useit.com [online]. Available from: <http://www.useit.com/alertbox/990307.html> (accessed 19.07.13.).

SUPR-Q: Standardized Universal Percentile Rank [online]. Available from: <http://www.suprq.com/> (accessed 21.04.13.).

RECOMMENDED READING

A Matter of Trust: What Users Want from Web Sites, 2002. [.pdf] Princeton Survey Research Associates, pp. 1—25. Available from: Consumers Union <http://consumersunion.org/wp-content/uploads/2013/05/a-matter-of-trust.pdf> (accessed 01.03.13.).

Corritore, C.L., Kracher, B., Wiedenbeck, S., 2003. On-line trust: concepts, evolving themes, a model. Int. J. Hum. Comput. Stud. 58 (6), 737—758.

Idler, S. (2011) Boost Your Web Credibility: Learn from the Pro's. Usabilla [blog] 26 February 2011. Available from: <http://blog.usabilla.com/credibility-trustworthiness-expertise/> (accessed 03.09.13.).

Riegelsberger, J., Sasse, M., McCarthy, J., 2003. Trust at First Sight? A Test of Users' Ability to Identify Trustworthy e-Commerce Sites, paper presented at HCI2003, 8—12 September 2003, Bath, UK, pp. 243—260.

Sauro, J., 2011. When credibility and trust matter more than usability. Measuring Usability [blog], 26 October 2011. Available from: <http://www.measuringusability.com/blog/credibility.php> (accessed 07.02.13.).

Wang, Y.D., Emurian, H.H., 2005. An overview of online trust: concepts, elements, and implications. Comput. Human Behav. 21 (1), 105—125.

CHAPTER 5

Beyond Web Site and UI Designs

While the vast majority of tests analyzed for this book dealt with web pages, and with singular design elements intended for web pages, there were numerous examples of tests that went "outside of the box." There are no limitations on what types of visual displays and materials can be tested using this method—recall that Section 2.4 describes a test featuring a snapshot of an ad posted on the back of a bus. It can be the right choice for any design issue involving perception of design elements and the emotions and responses they elicit, as long as the key principle is followed: *The five-second test is the wrong choice for anything requiring more than five seconds' worth of exposure in order to provide a meaningful answer.*

All of the rules and templates relative to target identification and attitudinal tests are viable for the following test scenarios. The memory dump format can also be used in all instances—just remember that viewers tend to focus on and report specific design elements first. Instructions that prompt the participant to "remember as much as you can" or to "let us know what parts jumped out at you" will virtually guarantee that specific elements—characters, logos, photos, colors, etc.—will be reported as the "things remembered."

5.1 DISPLAYS FOR TRADE SHOW BOOTHS/EXHIBITS

An effective trade show display will instantly grab the viewer's attention, promote the company or brand, communicate the product or service offered, and entice people to investigate further. A five-second test can be used to measure (among other things) prominence of the company/brand, memorability of the headline/tagline, obviousness of the product or service, and attitudinal aspects regarding visual appeal and/or emotional response.

Possible test questions for display tests (Figure 5.1)

- "What type of product is being sold?"
- "What type of person (or group of people) is this product targeted to?"

Figure 5.1 Product display example. Image used with permission by Shadow Beverage and Snacks.

- "What is the brand name of the product?"
- "The display is promoting a product for an 'Industrial Athlete.' What does the term 'Industrial Athlete' mean to you?"
- "Rate the display's visual appeal..."

5.2 PRINTED COLLATERAL AND ADVERTISEMENTS

Five-second tests can also be used to test the clarity, understandability, and aesthetic appeal of all kinds of virtual and printed collateral materials, including (but not limited to):

- Packaging
- Brochure pages
- Marketing materials
- Billboards
- Posters
- Doorknob hangers
- Business cards

- Table tents
- Resumes

Possible test questions for print materials

- "What company is featured in the ad?"
- "What type of product or service does the company provide?"
- "What does the ad recipient have a chance to win?"
- "Describe your reaction to the main image used in the ad."
- "In your opinion, is the main image an effective choice for this ad?"

5.3 POWERPOINT SLIDES

Aside from advice about the use of transitions and not reading a slide verbatim, lists of "biggest PowerPoint mistakes" typically warn against perceptual overload—too much information density, charts that are too busy, pictures used improperly, fonts that are the wrong size, ugly backgrounds, poor contrast between fonts and background, too many bullets, etc. Crowdsourced five-second tests are a great way to test the perceptual aspects of a slide, so that the key points of information communicated effectively.

Possible test questions for PowerPoint slides (Figure 5.2)

- "What is the main topic of the slide?"
- "What agency does the information come from?"
- "According to the graph, what is the general trend for carbon dioxide costs over the next 10 years?"
- "What incentive being offered to coal plants is noted in the slide?"

5.4 FORMS

One need go no further than the 2000 US presidential election to illustrate the potential consequences of improperly designed ballots and forms (Norden et al., 2008). Caroline Jarrett, a noted expert in the design of forms, has noted that if someone perceives a form as complex, it is (Jarrett and Gaffney, 2009). Five-second tests can help determine whether options align well with labels, required fields are obvious, information is presented optimally, and generally how complex a form is perceived to be (Figure 5.3).

Near-Term Power Plant Economics with CO$_2$ Allowance Costs

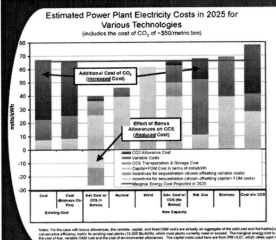

- To illustrate the economics of operating existing and new power technologies, the chart shows the cost of various technologies when the projected CO$_2$ allowance prices are included.

- Projected CO$_2$ allowance prices of roughly $50/ton in 2025 increase variable costs of existing plants powered by fossil fuels to the point where many are likely to shut down.

- However, S. 2191 provides significant incentives for CCS technology for coal plants in the form of bonus allowances, resulting in earlier penetration of advanced coal with CCS.

EPA Analysis of S. 2191

43

Figure 5.2 PowerPoint slide example.

Camden   A~Z | Accessibility | Site map | Contact | Help

The website of Camden Council,
at your service

🔍 Search

You are here: Home → Council and Democracy

Council and Democracy

Sign in

Register now

Resume a pending form

📝 **Register for my revenues and benefits**
Form reference: 5684549

Applicant

Please specify your business name in the 'any other names you are known by' field if relevant.

Items marked with an asterisk (*) must be completed.

Title	Select ▾
Forename 1	
Forename 2	
Forename 3	
Surname*	
Any other name you may be known by	
Address lookup	ⓘ Find... Clear Address Ref. ⓘ
Address*	
Town	
County	
Postcode	
Email address	

Page 1 of 5   Reset   Proceed >>

Figure 5.3 Online form example.

Possible test questions for forms

- "What is the purpose of this form?"
- "What (if any) fields are required to complete the form?"
- "What are the special instructions for business owners attempting to complete the form?"
- "Rate the complexity of this form..."
- "Based on the design, how difficult do you think the form is to complete?"

REFERENCES

Jarrett, C., Gaffney, G., 2009. Forms That Work. Morgan Kaufmann, Amsterdam.

Norden, L., Kimball, D., Quesenbery, W., Chen, M., 2008. *Better Ballots* [report]. Brennan Center for Justice at NYU School of Law, New York, NY, pp. 8–15.

Online Five-Second Test Tools

UsabilityHub: Five-Second Test

Available at www.usabilityhub.com, www.fivesecondtest.com

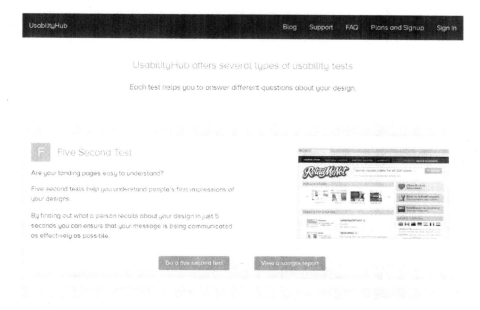

Figure A.1.1 www.usabilityhub.com.

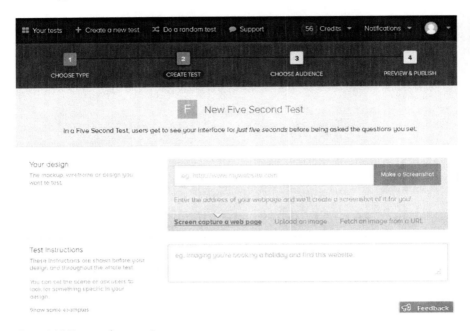

Figure A.1.2 Five-second test creation page.

Verify: Memory Test

Available at http://verifyapp.com/home

Figure A.1.3 http://verifyapp.com/home.

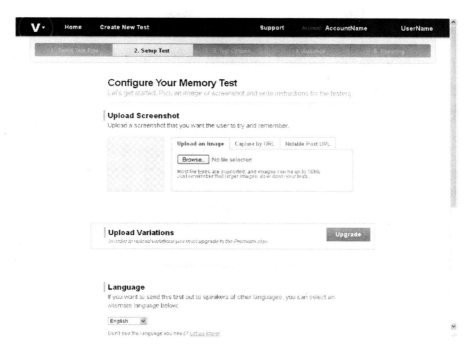

Figure A.1.4 Memory test creation page.

UserZoom: Screenshot Timeout Test

Available at http://www.userzoom.com/software/research-capabilities/screenshot-timeout-testing/

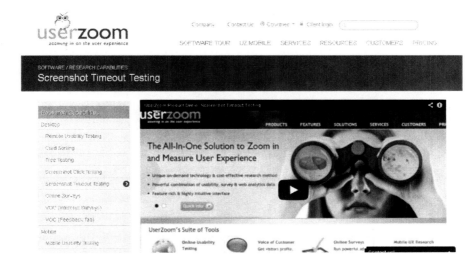

Figure A.1.5 http://www.userzoom.com.

Comparison Table

(information current as of the date of publication)

	Usability Hub.com	Verify	UserZoom
Test name	Five-second test	Memory test	Screenshot timeout test
Five-second test features	• Customize test instructions and questions • Easy image upload • Word cloud analysis of responses • "Karma points" crowdsourcing and social media link sharing • Participant demographics	• Customize test instructions • Language selection • Device selection • Open/closed test access • Custom test durations • Permissions for report access	• Customize test instructions and questions • Customize image exposure times • Integration into other types of testing • Advanced reporting/analytics
Other testing tools included	• Click testing • Navigation testing	• Preference test • Yes/no test • Click test • Multi Click test • Annotate test • Mood test • Label test	• Web Remote Usability testing • Mobile Usability testing • Card sorting • Tree testing • Screenshot Click testing • Online surveys
Subscription levels	• Community • Solo • Team • Studio • Agency	• Basic • Plus • Premium	• Basic • Pro • Enterprise
Price range	$0–$200/month	$19–$99/month	$9000/year and up

CPSIA information can be obtained at www.ICGtesting.com
Printed in the USA
BVOW04s0340280714

360608BV00010B/61/P